Lost Angels

UMETLO

In *Lost Angels*, Vicky Lebeau re-reads Freudian theories of femininity to develop a remarkable contribution to spectatorship theory. Lebeau discusses Freud's distinctive preoccupations with female fantasy and femininity – from his studies on hysteria and the 'family romance' at the origins of psychoanalysis to the analysis of mass psychology in the 1920s and 1930s. *Lost Angels* exposes how Freud's accounting of femininity is intimately tied to his changing representation of the paternal, and explores his ensuing differentiation between masculine and feminine fantasy through critical and feminist theories of spectatorship and cinema.

Discussing three popular 'youth' films of the 1980s – John Hughes's *Ferris Bueller's Day Off*, Francis Ford Coppola's *Rumble Fish* and Tim Hunter's *River's Edge* – Lebeau works through issues of sexual difference and social identification and creates a dialogue between feminism, psychoanalysis and the critical theory of the Frankfurt school. Intervening in current debates on femininity, fantasy and identification, Lebeau suggests that, for Freud, femininity is always both a sexed and a social category which cannot be understood outside of its relation to the father.

Lost Angels is a ground-breaking addition to current feminist film theory and essential reading for all students of film, gender and cultural studies.

Vicky Lebeau is Lecturer in English in the School of Cultural and Community Studies at the University of Sussex.

Frontispiece: production still from Robert Wiene's *The Cabinet of Dr. Caligari* (1919). Courtesy BFI.

Lost Angels

Psychoanalysis and cinema

Vicky Lebeau

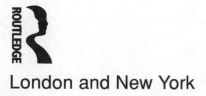

London and New York

First published 1995
by Routledge
11 New Fetter Lane, London EC4P 4EE

Simultaneously published in the USA and Canada
by Routledge
29 West 35th Street, New York, NY 10001

Typeset in Times by
Ponting–Green Publishing Services, Chesham, Bucks
Printed and bound in Great Britain by
TJ Press (Padstow) Ltd, Padstow, Cornwall.

British Library Cataloguing in Publication Data
A catalogue record for this book is available from the
British Library

Library of Congress Cataloging in Publication Data
Lebeau, Vicky.
  Lost Angels: psychoanalysis and cinema/Vicky Lebeau.
    p.   cm.
  Includes bibliographical references and index.
  1. Psychoanalysis and motion pictures.
  2. Motion pictures–psychological aspects.
  I. Title.
PN1995.9.P783L43   1994
791.43'01'9–dc20   94–11706

ISBN 0–415–10720–2
      0–415–10721–0 (pbk) ✓

For my family – especially DOREEN and
GARY LEBEAU

and

To the memory of my father,
TERRY LEBEAU
1939–1994

Contents

Acknowledgements

I would like to thank the following journals for permission to reprint (in revised form): '"You're my friend": *River's Edge* and social spectatorship', *Camera Obscura* and Indiana University Press; 'Daddy's Cinema', *Screen* and Oxford University Press. Acknowledgements also for permission to reprint from the following: *Less Than Zero* © 1985 by Bret Easton Ellis, reprinted by permission of Simon & Schuster, Inc. and Pan Macmillan; *Rumble Fish* by S.E. Hinton, by permission of Victor Gollancz; *The Culture of Narcissism, American Life in an Age of Diminishing Expectations*, by Christopher Lasch, by permission of W.W. Norton & Company, Inc. copyright © 1979 by Christopher Lasch; *Future Shock*, by Alvin Toffler, by permission of The Bodley Head.

My thanks to Jacqueline Rose and Rachel Bowlby for their commentary and support throughout the writing of this book, to John Shire for his friendship and for staying with the many different versions of these chapters and to Christine Blake for her generous reading at the critical moments. Thanks also to the women of the 'Sexual Difference: Women and Writing' seminar (Sussex, 1991) for their interest in S.E. Hinton and the 'masquerade'; and to Gary Lebeau for a fraternal gloss on *Rumble Fish*. For invaluable help, in different forms, my thanks to: the Graduate Colloquium, University of Sussex, Constance Penley, Nancy Wood, Doreen Lebeau, Terry Lebeau, Anne Crane, Peter Urpeth, Gwen Holmden, Vic Holmden, Paul Myerscough, Jo Croft, Richard Fuller and, for her (much appreciated) attempts to solve the enigma of 'the computer', Jane Phillips.

My special thanks, finally, to D.S. Marriott.

Chapter 1

Introduction

'One can learn nothing from them'

In 'Hysterical Phantasies and their Relation to Bisexuality', first published in 1908, Freud gave the following brief account of the 'favourable circumstances' in which a female patient was able to 'capture' an unconscious fantasy in the process of making its way into her conscious fantasy life or daydream:

> After I had drawn the attention of one of my patients to her phantasies, she told me that on one occasion she had suddenly found herself in tears in the street and that, rapidly considering what it was she was actually crying about, she had got hold of a phantasy to the following effect. In her imagination she had formed a tender attachment to a pianist who was well known in the town (though she was not personally acquainted with him); she had had a child by him (she was in fact childless); and he had then deserted her and her child and left them in poverty. It was at this point in her romance that she had burst into tears.
>
> (*Pelican Freud Library*, hereafter *PFL* 10: 88)

Curiously, however difficult it is for the daydreamer to become aware of and to reflect on the fantasmatic scenes which absorb her, it is only too obvious to others what she is doing – at least according to the description of the daydreamer's abstracted appearance in public that Freud gives just before this passage: 'It is easy to recognize a person who is absorbed in day-dreaming in the street, however, by his sudden, as it were absent-minded, smile, his way of talking to himself, or by the hastening of his steps which marks the climax of the imagined situation' (ibid.). We can compare this with the famous passage from the case history of Anna O. in *Studies on Hysteria* (1895) in which Joseph Breuer describes his patient's invisible participation in a 'private theatre':

This girl [Anna O.], who was bubbling over with intellectual vitality, led an extremely monotonous existence in her puritanically-minded family. She embellished her life in a manner which probably influenced her decisively in the direction of her illness, by indulging in systematic day-dreaming, which she described as her 'private theatre'. While everyone thought she was attending, she was living through fairy tales in her imagination; but she was always on the spot when she was spoken to, so that no one was aware of it. She pursued this activity almost continuously while she was engaged on her household duties, which she discharged unexceptionably. I shall presently have to describe the way in which this habitual day-dreaming while she was well passed over into illness without a break.

(*PFL* 3: 74)

Unlike the daydreamer walking through the streets, then, the woman at home, living out her life between the routine of household duties and the ennui of domestic leisure, gives no sign of her activity within – or, at least, not until daydreaming slides imperceptibly into illness. Everyone 'thought she was attending' while Anna O. ran through the scenes that, Breuer seems to imply, made the tedium of her life more tolerable. Because she was 'always on the spot when she was spoken to', no one could tell the difference, no one could tell that she was, in fact, not 'all there'. It is as if Anna O. really was in two places at once, responding to the voices that came at her from the outside at the same time as she was engaged in a self-to-self intimacy which, once revealed by what she was the first to describe as Breuer's 'talking cure', would be used as evidence of her double consciousness, of the difference within, whose effects psychoanalysis goes on to explain in terms of the unconscious.

In *Studies on Hysteria* the *appearance* of that difference, the point at which the unconscious makes its presence felt or manifest through the symptom, is intimately associated with the monotony stressed by both Freud and Breuer as a decisive element in the development of their patients' symptoms. In effect, and however variable the circumstances of these women's lives and histories, the hysteric daydreams because she is overtaken by the banality of her life – a link between fantasy and impoverishment which Freud continues to make throughout his work. 'We have nothing new to say on the question of the origin of these dispositional hypnoid states', he comments in the 'Preliminary Communication' of 1893, but '[t]hey often, it would seem, grow out of the day-dreams which are so common even to healthy people and to which needlework and similar occupations render women especially prone' (ibid.: 64). Though distraction is not its only form, *as* distraction fantasy works as something like a defence against reality by securing relief from boredom – in particular, it seems, for women. More than ten years later, in his discussion of the daydreamer in the street, Freud was still associating the activity of fantasy both with a sense of 'deprivation and longing' (*PFL* 10: 87) and with the sense of disempowerment that, in an analysis of the affective role of theatre in 'Psychopathic Characters on the Stage' (1905–6), he identified with the position of the spectator:

> The spectator is a person who experiences too little, who feels that he is a 'poor wretch to whom nothing of importance can happen', who has long been obliged to damp down, or rather displace, his ambition to stand in his own person at the hub of world affairs.
>
> (*PFL* 14: 121–2)

In its analysis of a public mode of fantasy production and consumption – of a public as opposed to a 'private theatre' – 'Psychopathic Characters' sketches the figure of a spectator dependent on both actor and playwright for the satisfaction of his wishes:

> [H]e longs to feel and to act and to arrange things according to his desires – in short, to be a hero. And the playwright and actor enable him to do this by allowing him to identify himself with a hero.
>
> (ibid.: 122)

In this case, a fantasy made public through a dramatic spectacle – Freud is always 'inclined' to believe that the creative writer presents us with his 'personal daydreams' (ibid.: 140) – moves in as an object of compensation for a spectator doubly displaced from both his 'ambitions' in the real world and the apparently more intimate or self-sufficient forms of daydreaming Freud describes elsewhere. While she ran her own theatre through her mind, Anna O. carried on working and remained more or less alert to the demands of the outside world. The daydreaming *flâneur* seemed oblivious to whatever was passing him by in the street. And somewhere between these two figures, the spectator finds him or herself succumbing to the preoccupying pleasures of a daydream that comes from someone else, that may never be quite his or her 'own' but which may even assuage that elusive sense of 'deprivation and longing' more effectively, more affectively, than his or her own. Freud seems certain, for example, that the consumption of other people's fantasies facilitates a type of derepression by presenting the reader/spectator with a sanctioned model for his or her own fantasy-life. The act of reading or looking is described as a form of 'forepleasure' which allows us to liberate 'greater pleasure arising from deeper psychical sources' otherwise subject to feelings of shame and so to repression: 'It may even be that not a little of this effect is due to the writer's enabling us thenceforward to enjoy our own day-dreams without self-reproach or shame' (*PFL* 14: 141).

'The subject of phantasies seems to have been very much on Freud's mind at about the date of this paper' according to the editor's introduction to 'Hysterical Phantasies' in 1908 (*PFL* 10: 86). At about the same time as he was examining these links between aesthetic production, consumption and daydreaming, Freud was also discussing the difficulty of psychoanalysing what, in a letter to Freud on 12 June 1907, Carl Jung had described as 'the uneducated':

> My outpatients' clinic is studded with thorns. Analysing the uneducated is a tough job. It is amusing to see how the female outpatients go about diagnosing each other's erotic complexes although they have no insight into their own. With uneducated patients the chief obstacle seems to be the atrociously crude transference.
>
> (McGuire 1974: 63)

Freud's reply to this letter picks up on the formation and function of fantasy in a way that starts to bring into focus the class position of the women treated by himself and Jung at this time:

> Of course you have hit the nail on the head with what you say about your ambulatory cases. What with their habits and mode of life, reality is too close to those women to allow them to believe in fantasies. If I had based my theories on the statements of servant girls, they would all be negative. And such behaviour fits in with other sexual peculiarities of that class; well-informed persons assure me that these girls are much less diffident about engaging in coitus than about being seen naked. Fortunately for our therapy, we have previously learned so much from other cases that we can tell these persons their story without having to wait for their contribution. They are willing to confirm what we tell them, but one can learn nothing from them.
>
> (ibid.: 64)

Nowhere, so far as I know, does Freud explicitly elaborate on these tantalizing comments about the fantasy life – or, more accurately, what seems to be the absence of a fantasy life – in women from the 'servant classes'. There are, though, a number of quite diverse contexts for these elliptic statements. The correspondence with Jung at this time, for example, is full of speculation about what Freud was describing as the 'fragility' (ibid.: 42) of the transference in schizophrenia as well as the 'atrociously crude transference' which Jung claimed to have identified in 'the uneducated'. There is, too, the question of who precisely the uneducated are here, a question which abuts onto the uncertain relation between psychoanalysis and education, or educability – Jung had already referred to the '"psychologically" educated [who] have blinkers before their eyes' when it comes to psychoanalysis (ibid.: 55). The scope of the problem is suggested by Freud's 'On Psychotherapy', delivered as a lecture before the College of Physicians in 1904. Setting out the conditions which indicate that psychoanalysis may have a beneficial effect for a particular patient, Freud described the 'determining factor of fitness' for psychoanalysis as 'whether the patient is educable' and went on to discuss that educability in terms of the patient's amenability to influence. Noting in passing that 'old people are no longer educable' because they are paralysed by a combination of memory and rigidity of the mental processes, Freud also suggested that 'there is very little room in the memory of the multitude' – a lack which, at least implicitly, disqualifies what he would later start to describe as 'the masses' from psychoanalysis as such. In fact, Freud spells it out: 'It is gratifying that precisely the most valuable and most highly developed persons are best suited for these curative measures' (Freud 1963: 70–4).

It is in this context – a context which is not easily separable from the narcissistic gratifications of psychoanalysis with itself – that Freud makes an elision between servant girls and 'the uneducated' and, in effect, turns working women into the thorn in the side of psychoanalysis. Crucially, as he does so, he embeds in his theory of fantasy a distinction between two types of reality. The pressure of a reality from which, classically, the bored hysteric finds relief in daydreaming is here qualified by a reality that kills fantasy – or, more precisely, by a reality which kills the affect of fantasy. Freud does not quite say that there is an absence of fantasy in the lives of working women. He leaves open the possibility that the servant girls have fantasies but don't believe in them: '[R]eality is too close to those women to allow them to believe in fantasies. If I had based my theories on the statements of servant girls, they would all have been negative.' Again, there is an ambiguity in this statement: have the servant girls told Freud stories which negate the classical forms of fantasy discovered through the analyses of the hysterics – the fantasy, crudely, of having been sexually seduced by the father? Have they simply denied the existence, or importance, of fantasy? Or is it that Freud can find no form of daydreaming and fantasizing as such in the lives of these women? These questions remain strictly undecidable on the evidence of this short letter. What we can say is that Freud has reinflected the problem – familiar to psychoanalysis from its inception – of how to make the distinction between fantasy and reality. In a now famous, if not infamous, letter to his friend and colleague Wilhelm Fliess in 1897, Freud set out his doubts about the truth of the accounts of sexual assault and seduction told to him by his hysterical patients – accounts on which he had based his theory of the hysterical symptom as the effect of the repressed memory of a sexual assault. Faced with another type of negation of his psychoanalysis, Freud stressed his bewilderment to Fliess: '[T]here are no indications of reality in the unconscious, so that one cannot distinguish between truth and fiction that has been cathected with affect . . . Now I have no idea of where I stand' (cited by Masson 1984: 108–9). The fantasy lives of the servant girls, however, introduce a new difficulty. In this new case, we have to tell the difference not only between fantasy and reality but between real, affective and absorbing fantasy lives and 'fake' or disaffected ones. However we might make this distinction, Freud is clear that it has some bearing on the behaviour and the 'sexual peculiarities' of the servant girls who, it seems, do not mediate their sexuality through the family romance or the seduction fantasy – a failure that threatens to negate both psychoanalytic theory and practice: 'If I had based my theories on the statements of servant girls, they would all have been negative.'

A sense that we are not far away from the vicissitudes of the seduction theory and the uncertain distinctions between reality and fantasy indissociable from the mutual implication of memory, fantasy and the real event in Freud's work is reinforced by his concluding comments to Jung on the use-value of the servant women's fantasies: 'They are willing to confirm what we tell them, but one can learn nothing from them.' Here Freud is repeating, almost word for word, the advice he had given to Jung on the treatment of a 6-year-old girl just a few weeks before. Jung had written to Freud with a brief outline of the case on 13 May 1907:

At the moment I am treating a 6-year-old girl for excessive masturbation and lying after alleged seduction by her foster-father. Very complicated! . . . Except for a colourless and affect-less, totally ineffectual representation of the trauma in conscious-ness, I have not succeeded in obtaining any abreaction with affect, either spontaneous or suggested. At present it looks as if the trauma were a fake. Yet where does the child get all those sexual stories from?

(McGuire 1974: 45)

Harking back to the 'complicated' cases of incestuous assault which had been presented to Freud in the 1880s and 1890s, Jung's vexed question about the source of the young girl's 'sexual stories' also inevitably recalls the obscure origins of sexual knowledge which dominated Freud's (again famously) failed analysis of 'Dora'. But his reply to Jung is supremely confident:

In your six-year-old girl, you must surely have discovered in the meantime that the attack is a fantasy that has become conscious, something which is regularly disclosed in analysis and which misled me into assuming the existence of generalized traumas in childhood. The therapeutic task consists in demonstrating the sources from which the child derives its sexual knowledge. *As a rule children provide little information but confirm what we have guessed when we tell them.* Questioning of the families indispens-able. When it is successful, the most delightful analyses result.

(ibid.: 48; my italics)

There seems to be no trace of an agony of indecision here. The girl's hysterical attack is simply a fantasy which has become conscious and which threatens to lure Jung, the unsuspecting analyst, into misread-ing it as the mnemic symbol of a repressed trauma, a real sexual assault. Thus there is no question about what Jung has to do. Like the servant girls, children will confirm what they are told – even, perhaps, believe what they are told? – and all that the analyst needs to show is the origin of their sexual knowledge.

The analyst's task, then, consists in answering the question that Jean Laplanche and Jean-Bertrand Pontalis discover behind the fantasy of seduction itself: 'Where does her sexuality come from?' In the correspondence with Jung, however, Freud's advice on how to answer that question seems to lose sight of the undecidable borderline, crucial to the seduction theory, between a sexuality belonging within – belonging, in a sense, to the subject herself – and a sexuality which erupts violently within the subject from the outside. (This is discussed in more detail in Chapter 3.) The letter to Jung seems to introduce a different kind of uncertainty. On the one hand, if it is the child's unconscious fantasy life (and not a real event) which is generating the hysterical attack, what sense does it make to 'question the family'? What kind of unconscious and what kind of fantasy life is it that has to be checked against what the family knows and says? On the other hand, if Freud means simply that Jung should verify what the child has said about her sexual knowledge by comparing her story with the one told by her family, then he is recommending an essential depletion of the psychoanalytic method itself. Instead of an analysis which works through the child's transference onto the analyst, we have an investigation into the sources of sexual knowledge which can be undertaken, in its essentials, outside of the relation between the analyst and the analysand. That depletion may have to do with Freud's reservations about the psychoanalysis of children as such. If so – and it's worth recalling the difference of his 'analysis', albeit via the father, of Little Hans – those reservations are clearly not confined to children but extend to the servant girls who can also do nothing but confirm the truth of what Freud has 'guessed' about them, the truth of the 'delightful analyses' which result from a story known inside out.

In one sense, then, it is the aesthetics of the psychoanalytic procedure that is at issue in these analyses of children and servants. But, and intriguingly, the more 'delightful', complete and coherent the stories being passed between analyst and patient, so the more incoherent the theoretical account of psychoanalytic technique seems to become. As we've seen, that incoherence shows up in the curiously public unconscious ascribed to the child. It is there, too, in Freud's description of the difficulties specific to analysing servant girls which starts with the problem of what appears to be the absence of a fantasy life recognizable to psychoanalysis and ends by claiming that psychoanalysis has learned so much from other cases that it is possible to 'tell these persons their story'. In order to make this move, though, Freud has to renege on one of the essential insights of psychoanalysis – insights being worked out between himself and Jung in their discussions about the labour of transference and resistance in any successful analysis which depends on the therapeutic importance of the patient's affective speech. Something about what the servant girls say, or fail to say, makes Freud forget the evidently strenuous labour of the psychoanalytic technique, provoking him, instead, into finding solace in the pleasures of a known and familiar story.

It could be said that what Freud closes down here – what his class and sex prejudice closes down – is the possibility of another story, another set of fantasies and narratives that just might have been different to those he was used to hearing. It is a closure which can only confirm a pervasive sense that however central women have been as analysts, as analysands and as objects of both erotic and theoretical fantasy in the development of psychoanalysis, the more or less loving, more or less seductive, alliances between feminism and psychoanalysis are not for all women. Elizabeth Abel summarizes a familiar set of criticisms at the beginning of her recent essay, 'Race, Class, and Psychoanalysis? Opening Questions':

Seduced by psychoanalytic accounts of subjectivity, most feminist theory of the 1970s has come to seem, from the vantage point of the late 1980s, to have lost its material groundings and with them the possibility of interpreting (and thereby promoting) social change. The traditional indifference of psychoanalysis to racial, class, and cultural differences, and the tendency of psychoanalysis to insulate subjectivity from social practices and discourses all run contrary to a feminism increasingly attuned to the power of social exigencies and differences in the constitution of subjectivity.

(Abel 1990: 184)

A claim that the seductions of psychoanalysis can only lead us – women, feminists – up a white and suburban garden path is ubiquitous, even from feminists sympathetic to the specificity of what psychoanalysis may have to say about that disarmingly familiar 'constitution of subjectivity'. In *Landscape for a Good Woman*, for example, the feminist historian Carolyn Steedman assesses psychoanalysis as an interpretative tool which foregrounds the psychosexual complexity of the middle-class woman and then ignores the psychical and social realities of the working classes. For Steedman, 'the original subjects of psychoanalytic case-study' are allowed 'an active role in the production of historical evidence, whilst the much larger number of people to whom it is suggested these understandings are passed on, are seen simply as the passive objects of transmission' (Steedman 1986: 76). This is not to say, Steedman continues, that the psychoanalytic framework cannot be used across class barriers; the fact that it can be so used, despite economic, social and historical differences 'is to do with the desire to be part of a story, even if it is someone else's' (ibid.: 77).

The purchase of Steedman's account makes itself felt alongside that shift from disbelief to confirmation identified by Freud in the servant girls' reactions to fantasies. We can read his claim that the servant girls are only too willing to accept his version of their history as proof of a desire to inhabit a story, any story – even if, as Steedman suggests, the psychoanalytic narrative on offer cannot use the 'stuff of the world . . . streets, food, work, dirt' presumably more familiar to these women than the jewel-cases, pearl ear-rings, nurse-maids and leisurely inertia which figure so centrally in Freud's most famous psychoanalytic case histories (ibid.: 77). But, and in a way that is perhaps problematic, Steedman's emphasis on the story that doesn't fit the model, the story which fails to be told or, if told, heard, suggests that the story is at least there, waiting to be told, if only we knew how to listen to and decipher it. Implicitly, an extension or multiplication of narratives and a fine-tuning of psychoanalytic listening would allow the servant girls to tell Freud whatever it is they wish or know. This is close to that moment in the development of psychoanalysis when an ability to give a coherent account of oneself is taken as a sign of psychic health – when the hysterical symptom is matched up with the gaps and amnesias in the hysteric's speech. In this sense, it is as if when Freud denies working-class women access to a fantasy-life of their own, that fantasy-life starts to take on the status of a suppressed or censored truth, of a historical reality which, in turn, becomes easily inseparable from a desire to rediscover and to return whatever it is that has been mutilated or destroyed – something which continues to agitate precisely to the extent that we cannot hear it.

One of the effects of this investment in narrative is to lose sight of the constant and interminable disruption of knowledge – of the ability to account for oneself – introduced by the psychoanalytic account of the unconscious. This forgetting of the unconscious mirrors Freud's own forgetting, the forgetting of psychoanalysis taking place through the correspondence with Jung – at least when the psychoanalysis of children or servant girls is at issue. To put this slightly differently: at this juncture between sex, class and fantasy, psychoanalysis could be said to perform a type of occupation of its subjects, to occupy and so to violate or destroy the fantasies which

are supposed to be the privileged objects of psychoanalytic discourse. At the same time, if there is a violation here it is not confined
to the objects of psychoanalysis. Freud does not only forget the
decisive role played by the analysand's affective speech in the
psychoanalytic cure; he also succumbs to what, three years later with
the publication of 'Wild Psychoanalysis', he would describe as a
'wild' or popular abuse of psychoanalysis itself. In 1906, Jung had
warned Freud that 'the more psychoanalysis becomes known, the
more will incompetent doctors dabble in it and make a mess of it.
This will then be blamed on you and your theory' (McGuire 1974:
11). In 'The Psychoanalytic Movement', in 1914, Freud acknowledged the reservations he had had about the increasing popularity of
his work: 'I considered it necessary to form an official association
because I feared the abuses to which psychoanalysis would be
subjected as soon as it became popular' (*PFL* 15: 102). The young,
suburban physician of 'Wild Psychoanalysis' stands accused of just
such a scientific and technical misunderstanding of psychoanalysis.
According to Freud, 'he understands the expression "sexual life"'
in 'the popular sense' of coitus. Further, he too has made the mistake
of simply telling his patient – a woman, recently divorced and
suffering from anxiety states – the cause of her symptoms: sexual
frustration. Freud is, in this case, adamant:

> The idea that a neurotic is suffering from a sort of ignorance, and
> that if one removes this ignorance by telling him facts (about the
> causal connection of his illness with his life, about his experiences
> in childhood, and so on) he must recover, is an idea that has long
> been superseded, and one derived from superficial appearances.
> (Freud 1963: 93)

This misappropriation of his theory and technique brings Freud up
against what it would mean for psychoanalysis to be popular – a
popularity represented here by the amateur enthusiast who rushes in
with neither the tools nor the training and has then to call on Freud
to undo the damage of his work. The cause for concern is the
symptom of a woman who comes to ask for reassurance from Freud
that she is not incurable even though the three therapeutic alter-
natives suggested by the physician – returning to her husband, taking
a lover or masturbation – strike her as either impossible or repugnant.
The friend who accompanies the patient – described by Freud as 'a
still older, pinched and unhealthy-looking woman' – also implores
him to confirm the young doctor's mistake: 'It could not possibly be

true, for she herself had been a widow for many years, and had remained respectable without suffering from anxiety' (ibid.: 90).

It's worth noticing that when anxiety becomes a symptom of respectability, a sign of the woman who does not give way to the desire to satisfy herself sexually, so the reputations of psycho-analysis and the woman become intriguingly and inextricably linked. 'Wild Psychoanalysis' is a statement of reassurance to all of us – women – that the 'danger to patients and to the cause of psychoanalysis' (ibid.: 95) represented by the dabblers and dilet-tantes is being combated from within the International Psycho-analytical Association founded in 1910. In fact, as Freud makes clear at the end of the article, its popularity is more of a threat to psychoanalysis than to individual patients. The wild psychoanalyst did, after all, direct the woman's attention to the 'real cause of her trouble, or in that direction, and in spite of all her struggles that cannot be without some favourable results' (ibid.: 95). We have to look elsewhere, then, for what really troubles Freud about the physician's intervention:

> Oddly enough, the three therapeutic alternatives of this would-be psychoanalyst leave no room for – psychoanalysis! This woman can only be cured of her anxiety by returning to her husband, or by satisfying her needs by onanism or with a lover. And where does analytic treatment come in, the treatment which we regard as the first remedy in anxiety-states?
>
> (ibid.: 93)

Better than a husband, better than a lover or the auto-erotic pleasures of masturbation, psychoanalysis takes up its place as something akin to the lost half of the woman, carving out a primary and loving space for itself defined against the imperfections of a popular and second-rate technique. Above all, then, what the 'popular' physician has forgotten is psychoanalysis – just as, when he is confronted with the servant girls, Freud forgets himself and sees nothing but the popular act of coitus: '[W]ell-informed persons assure me that these girls are much less diffident about engaging in coitus than about being seen naked.' Passing over what they might have to say about that diffidence, he tells 'these girls' a story about their fantasy; or rather, he tells them his story about someone else's fantasy as if it were their own and then asks them to confirm it.

Not least because we are told that the servant girls are 'happy' to oblige, it is this request which opens psychoanalysis up to the charge of at best not listening to, or at worst taking over the fantasy lives of its 'working-class' subjects. In this sense, the servant girls represent a limit point for the development of Freud's theory and technique. 'I am glad to hear that your Russian girl is a student', Freud wrote to Jung towards the end of 1906 in reply to the latter's brief account of the early stages of his treatment of Sabine Spielrein, 'uneducated persons are at present too inaccessible for our purposes' (McGuire 1974: 8). For Jung, the answer to this inaccessibility, the alternative to psychoanalysis, is hypnosis – 'Most uneducated hysterics are unsuitable for psychanalysis. I have had some bad experiences here. Occasionally hypnosis gets better results' (ibid.: 11) – a return to the renounced procedures at the origin of psycho-analysis which Freud had, in fact, always found more suitable for patients from the lower social classes. In a discussion of the use of hypnotism in Bernheim's clinic, for example, which he visited in 1889, Freud drew attention to the efficacy of Bernheim's practice of treating patients in large, frequently spectacular, groups. The patients, by watching the effects of hypnosis on other people, can learn by imitation how to behave. She – and it is 'she' in this account – falls into a state of 'psychical preparedness' which facilitates her 'fall into deep hypnosis as soon as [her] turn comes'. The only drawback is that 'the ailments of each individual are discussed before a large crowd, which would not be suitable with patients of a higher social class' (*Standard Edition*, hereafter *SE* 1: 107–8).

Thus the public form of hypnosis and group mimesis set out by Freud before his turn to the more private practice of psychoanalytic free association and transference-love still affords 'better results' for the lower classes seventeen years later. The transference-love, or atrocious lack of it, at issue here is not only, as Jung would have it, the transference-love not shown by the lower classes. The trans-ference-love of the analyst is also in question. 'Various qualifications are demanded in the person if he is to be beneficially affected by psychoanalysis', Freud insists again in 1904, 'a certain measure of natural intelligence and ethical development may be required of him; with worthless persons the physician soon loses the interest which makes it possible for him to enter profoundly into the mental life of the patient' (Freud 1963: 60). In practice, it seems, psychoanalysis cannot love everyone enough to listen to them, let alone enough to cure them. The old, the uneducated and the servant girls cannot benefit from what Freud calls the 'cure . . . effected by love' because they do not love psychoanalysis and psychoanalysis does not love them (McGuire 1974: 13). Which is not to say that they cannot be hypnotized by one another.

As these oppositions emerge through the correspondence between Freud and Jung and in the papers on technique published by Freud between 1904 and 1910, it becomes evident that when psychoanalysis is forgotten, when it forgets itself, it inevitably deforms both its theory and its practice – and perhaps forgetting too is inevitable. That deformation, associated not only with his 'wild' or misguided followers but with Freud himself, then leads to the type of habitual – or perhaps ideological – interpretation exemplified in Freud's response to the servant girls. In this case, what is most troubling about Freud's analysis of the servant girls is his willingness to use a familiar and stereotypical account of fantasy to fill up a gap which threatens to appear, to speak quickly and so to stop something else from being said. This is, all too obviously, a refusal of specificity and of difference which lays bare the movement of an imposition of a fantasy structure on a sex and a class as perceived within psychoanalysis at this stage. However different, however challenging, psychoanalysis may have been, and may still be, its capacity to frame its objects through its naturalized stories about seduction, about Oedipus, about sexual difference and phylogenesis is always open to the risk of a banality which seems to mirror the monotony and repetition from which Freud and Breuer started in their analyses of hysteria. In other words, the more convincingly it tells its stories, the more effectively it applies its techniques, the more psychoanalysis risks becoming its own symptom. The appropriative gesture which refuses, or is unable, to theorize the difference between the hysterical fantasy which moves in as a response to the tedium of reality and the apparent loss of fantasy caused by a reality which is 'too close' is indissociable from the one which cannot hear what the servant girls might say, which fails to represent the specificity of their reality.

At the same time, Freud's retreat into habitual psychoanalysis leaves us with the ambivalent theoretical legacy of a desire to discover something that seems to have been lost but may, in fact, never have been, to retrieve from the forgetting performed by psychoanalysis something about the fantasmatic and transferential processes – structures and objects – which appear to have been denied. We are left, too, suspended between the explanatory force of psychoanalysis and its evident capacity to preoccupy us, to inhabit us to the point of our confirming the story it tells whether we believe in it or not – a suspension which leaves us in an uneasy and ambiguous state of indecision between psychoanalysis as the means to a critique and psychoanalysis as the object of a critique. There is also a third possibility or potential – which does not resolve but adds to the ambivalence – of psychoanalysis as auto-critique. Turning psychoanalysis against itself, as we've seen, shows up the pressure points of its own constitution as a discourse which aims to account for the dislocating effects of fantasy and of the unconscious. And those pressure points, in turn, can be used to identify the difficulties encountered by psychoanalysis as a theory of fantasy and of the unconscious.

The elaboration of the formation and function of fantasy and daydream running through the texts I've discussed in this Introduction could be said to oscillate between a more or less aesthetic appreciation of the benevolent effects of a daydream made both communal and dramatic via the creative gifts of the writer and a more silent, less speakable, participation in a fantasy structure which is able to stake its claim in its audience – whether in the name of the pleasures of dramatic identifications that we could not produce for ourselves or of narratives which tell a story about our otherwise inexplicable and bewildering symptoms. Very schematically, a sense of unease at the story about the servant girls who so readily inhabit the narrative Freud tells so confidently from within psychoanalysis casts doubt on the pleasures of the spectator who can identify as a hero by participating in a public daydream. It is as if the juxta-position of these different figures highlights certain key words from Freud's brief analysis of spectatorship: the spectator as a 'poor wretch', dampening down or displacing his 'ambition', or to push the point, his omnipotent fantasies, until he finds them reproduced somewhere outside himself; the shame and concealment char-acterizing daydreams until they find moral and aesthetic reinforce-ment, once again from outside; and finally, the 'deprivation and longing' motivating fantasy as such, enabling those other, more public forms of daydreaming to mediate and to take up their place within our fantasy lives.

It is at this point that a question about the habitual, or what Breuer called the 'systematic', nature of fantasy comes back (*PFL* 3: 74). For Breuer, Anna O.'s symptom seems to have had as much to do with the fact that she daydreamed *systematically* as with the existence of the unconscious, of fantasy, itself: 'She embellished her life in a manner which probably influenced her decisively in the direction of her illness, by indulging in systematic day-dreaming, which she described as her "private theatre"' (ibid.: 74). Put this way, there is an irresistible coincidence between Breuer's anxiety about the fixated and compensatory fantasy indulged in by his patient and the types of pessimism and anxiety which run alongside the development of mass cultural forms, frequently focusing on the effects of the 'dream factories' – the effects, that is, of a type of systematized fantasy – on individual and collective forms of fantasy life. That anxiety has isolated a set of persistent questions which will be taken up at different points through the analyses of cinema, spectatorship and fantasy in this book. At the same time, if only because we can see psychoanalysis in the process of blinding itself with its own obviousness at the junctures between sex and class, between fantasy and the 'popular', the readings of and through Freud's theory of fantasy, of femininity and of collectivity put forward in the following chapters remain subject to an oscillation, or an uncertainty, about the status of psychoanalysis as an object of or means to a critique. Any reading of Freud has to be selective but I want also to acknowledge a type of decision in the trajectory I've decided to follow through his work. Briefly, I've chosen to focus on those texts that allow us to make a set of associations between Freud's theory of femininity and his analysis of melancholia, between the accounts of the masculine and social superego and the analyses of a feminine and mass form of social degradation in relation to the paternal function. What emerges, in turn, from these associations is a way of thinking about a coincidence between the mass and the feminine in Freud's texts as the effect of a form of preoccupied or fixated fantasy life – a preoccupation which can then be used to examine the logic of social and fantasmatic dispossession which supports the different critiques of the mass and the feminine spectator in feminist and critical theories of film.

That axis – social identification and its malaise/mass culture and the female spectator – brings the problem of the female spectator into contact with a critique of mass culture at the juncture between cinematic and social identification. The section on 'Daddy's Cinema' explores the accounts of mass and feminine identifications in cinema and the social through the 'dilemmas' of the female spectator which have been so central to a psychoanalytically oriented feminist film theory and the victimized figure of the spectator which emerges through the analyses of the culture industry put forward by the Frankfurt School – in particular, Theodor Adorno, Max Horkheimer

and, more recently, Alexander Kluge. These different but intimately
connected criticisms describe a form of spectatorship which can be
used to question a critical and public dismissal of a contemporary
mainstream youth cinema (the 'brat pack' films associated with
John Hughes) and its spectators for their representations of, and
participation within, an infantilizing and debasing collective fantasy
life. Some of these issues reappear in the section on Francis
Coppola's *Rumble Fish*. The main focus here, though, is the
disturbance introduced into the fantasmatic figure of Narcissus and
the fantasy of masculine group identification worked through him
(a figure and a fantasy invested, in different ways, by Freud, by film
theory and by Coppola's film) by the presence, both on and off
screen, of the woman who wrote the novel on which *Rumble Fish*
is based, Susan Hinton.

As we shall see, running parallel with Freud's account of the
category of the feminine as the effect of a preoccupation with the
father (which takes the form, finally, of a real demand for his love)
is her exclusion from the socializing tie to Narcissus – a tie which
depends on the institution of an alliance between brothers through
the libidinized fiction of paternal love. On the one hand, that
exclusion requires the woman to use her bisexuality, to identify
across sexual difference, if she is to participate in Freud's fantasy of
the social alliance as a fraternal tie derived from the murder of a
primal father. On the other hand, it makes her prone to a type of
dereliction in her relation to the social, a dereliction which has to do
with the way in which the woman can be excluded into spectatorship
– she is nothing but the passive and supportive spectator of an active
masculinity. Both exclusion and dereliction are given another and
fatal twist by Tim Hunter's *River's Edge*, which starts from the real
event of the murder, in 1981, of a young woman by a fellow student
who then boasted of the killing and took his friends out to see the
body. The social disaffection supposed to characterize a 'new
generation' of youth underlies the film's examination of the collective aspect of spectatorship and of what the spectator can be asked
to symbolize on behalf of cinema.

Finally, all this is not to pit an authentic form of fantasizing or
daydreaming which would belong to, or properly delineate, the
boundaries of the individual against an occupied and degraded mode
of fantasy bearing witness to something like a lack of imagination
or identity. On the contrary, psychoanalysis, and in particular its
theory of transference, is effectively undermining the possibility of

establishing that type of distinction with any degree of certainty or legitimacy. How can we tell whether the family romance is a fantasy belonging to Freud or to the well-to-do, educated hysteric? And from what Freud tells us, are we sure that that fantasy does not also belong, along with any number of undescribed others, to the lower-class girls who eventually subscribe to it? Above all, perhaps, fantasy becomes a process of exchange, or is constructed and represented through an exchange which confuses the type of self-to-self intimacy so easily associated with it. Far from being our most cherished and 'intimate possessions' (*PFL* 14: 133), fantasies become the privileged site of our engagement with an outside which is simultaneously an engagement with the other's fantasy and with the other as fantasy.

Chapter 2

Daddy's cinema

Femininity and mass spectatorship

At the very end of John Hughes's *Ferris Bueller's Day Off* (1986), Ferris comes back on screen to make his final address to the film's spectators: 'You're still here? It's over. Go home. Go!' Thus a surprised question and an impatient command – 'Go!' – are used to signal that Ferris is no longer colluding, or playing, with the audience as he has been throughout the film. Suddenly there is a limit – an end, a conclusion – which we, the spectators, in our bid to extend the pleasures of cinema, have failed to recognize. We are – again, suddenly – in the wrong place at the wrong time, guilty of trespass, of staying too long, and so of outstaying our welcome: 'You're still here?'

On the one hand, the final frames of the film recall both a Brechtian aesthetic of interruption and defamiliarization and what Barbara Creed describes as the 'surface knowingness and playfulness' of the popular postmodern (Creed 1988: 97). On the other hand (and what I want to focus on here), there is a sense in which these frames evoke a spectator who, by ignoring or misrecognizing the boundaries of the film, has asked too much of cinema and has been, rather ungently, turned away. It is a dismissal which, in turn, suggests an intrusive or violating demand for something from the fiction put up by the film, a demand that immediately goes beyond the space and temporality of cinema and drifts into the real world: 'You're still here?'

It is not surprising, perhaps, that a desire to sustain the fictions and images of cinema beyond the cinema itself has been coded as both feminine and adolescent. Angela McRobbie, for example, has commented on the 'panorama of visuality focusing on male good looks' which dominates the teen magazines aimed at girls and young women for whom the beautiful (male) faces of cinema and pop music

– among them the actor who plays Ferris, Matthew Broderick – are commodified and circulated as objects of fantasy (McRobbie 1991: 154). *Ferris* could even be said to acknowledge, and confirm, this coding through the figure of the jealous and vengeful sister, Jeannie. Constantly threatening to expose Ferris's illicit 'day off', Jeannie is finally reconciled to her brother by a brief encounter with a beautiful and anonymous delinquent, played by Charlie Sheen (another of the 'teen pin-ups' popular in the mid-1980s). Implicitly accepting Sheen's diagnosis of her guilt – 'Your problem's not your brother. Your problem's you' – Jeannie renounces her envious dislike of Ferris and becomes, like almost everyone else in the film, one of his fans. But Jeannie's status as a fan is doubled. Overwhelmed by a kiss from Charlie Sheen, she represents the generic type of the *female fan* – the paradigmatic instance of a femininity seduced by a spectacle of masculinity to which it hysterically succumbs.

In one sense, then, *Ferris* profiles briefly within its narrative the tantalized spectatorship which seems to be solicited by its final frames, a spectatorship which is both gendered and placed within a family romance. The spectator who stays too long, who asks too much, is like a sister who doesn't seem to know when she isn't wanted, who carries on playing long after the game is over. As she does so, she leaves herself open to the accusation that she has got it wrong, that she is foolishly mistaken in what she has asked for from the fiction she has been inhabiting through the film. Found, and left, wanting, she can do nothing but leave the scene of her errant demand: 'You're still here? It's over. Go home. Go!'

John Hughes has been described as one of the most successful film directors of the 1980s – from *Sixteen Candles* (1984), through *The Breakfast Club* (1984) and *Weird Science* (1985) to *Ferris Bueller's Day Off* (1986) and, more recently, *Home Alone* (1990). He produced and scripted *Pretty in Pink* (directed by Howard Deutch) in 1986. But what first struck me about the placing of the spectator through the final frames of *Ferris Bueller's Day Off* was the way in which it seemed to repeat a more general critical reproach to the 'simple-minded', or deluded, audience for Hughes's films. The 'joke' about his girlfriend's enforced abortion made by the murderous narrator of Bret Easton Ellis's *American Psycho* is only the most obvious example:

At the airport I instruct the chauffeur to stop at F.A.O. Schwarz before picking Jeanette up and purchase the following: a doll, a rattle, a teething ring, a white Gund polar bear, and have them sitting in the backseat for her, unwrapped. Jeanette should be okay – she has her whole life in front of her (that is, if she doesn't run into me). Besides this girl's favorite movie is *Pretty in Pink* and she thinks Sting's cool, so what is happening to her is, like, not totally undeserved and one shouldn't feel bad for her. This is no time for the innocent.

(Ellis 1991: 381–2)

This passage is remarkable for its splicing of a disavowable aggressivity with a recognition-effect generated by the reference to the cultural redundancy of those who enjoy Hughes's films. Compare the *Time Out* reviews of *Ferris Bueller's Day Off* and *The Breakfast Club*:

Ferris . . . is a boy who gets anything he wants, screws over anyone who gets in his way, and gets patted on the back for doing so . . . [an] admittedly entertaining, at times delightful fellow. How unfortunate that no one got to wring the little bastard's neck.

(Goldman 1989: 198)

[T]he characters drone on about themselves and their puerile problems en route to emerging as fully paid-up members of the Me Generation . . . Characters who beef about not being taken seriously as real people would cut more ice were they not merely clothes-horses for crudely defined teen tribalism and strings of social clichés. *The Big Chill* served up again for the Simple-Minded set.

(Billson 1989: 75)

This is an account of Hughes's cinema as the symptom of a youth culture which is both self-obsessed and anomic, a cinema and a culture which has betrayed the youth rebellions of the 1960s and 1970s – 'Simple Minds' being coded here, I think, as a 'sold-out' punk band. In other words, Hughes's spectators are Thatcher's children, or, more precisely, the children of a political and economic alliance between Ronald Reagan and Margaret Thatcher, and they stand accused of a cinematic, aesthetic and, above all, a political banality. Kathryn Flett has suggested that Hughes found the 'perfect cinematic formula for the mid-Eighties': kids *as kids*, 'kids who hang out with other kids rather than playing – however convincingly – at being adults' (Flett 1989: 17). In the 'clean teen pics' or the 'brat pack' films of the 1980s, she continues, there are no Lolitas, no Christiane F.s, no Jodie Fosters (no sexuality, no drug-taking, no delinquency) – an omission which Flett refers back to a demand made by 'Reagan's America' and so to the perfect circle of a politically reactionary decade and a cinema of facile and materialistic conservatism.

Thus the fans of this cinema can become the objects of an easy derision passing between the different critical sites represented by, for example, Bret Easton Ellis's 'psycho', a public and parodic critique of Hughes's cinema and, at least in the case of *Ferris Bueller's Day Off*, that cinema itself. At the same time, the clamour of what has been described as the 'I want it now' generation seems to find its silent echo in the spectator who stays behind after the credits to see what else she might get – an echo which, in turn, sets up an association between the neutral mass of spectators subsumed by commercial cinema and a female, or feminized, spectator dazzled, fixated, by what she has seen.

The axis between the mass/youth and the female spectator, and the profound disrespect it seems to provoke, brings into focus a problem, for me, in the category of the spectator for film theory. In fact, the figure of the dazzled or occupied spectator represents a crucial link between recent feminist analyses of the dilemmas of the female spectator and a critique of cinema as a mass cultural form seducing its spectators into degraded types of collective identification. The mass and the feminine, the social and the sexual, come together in film theory in a spectator associated both with a legacy of cultural pessimism running alongside the development of mass cultural forms and a feminist analysis of, and discontent with, the masochistic, masculine or marginalized identifications available to the female spectator (Stacey 1987: 48). In 'Woman as Sign', her influential reading of Claude Lévi-Strauss's analysis of women as the privileged objects of social exchange, for example, Elizabeth Cowie cites the following brief passage from Sharon Smith's 'The Image of Women in Film', first published in 1972, in which Smith describes a 'self-respecting' female spectator: 'Women, as a fully human form, have almost completely been left out of film . . . That is, from its very beginning they were present but not in characterizations any self-respecting person could identify with' (Cowie 1978: 49). Only the image of a 'fully human' woman, it seems, would allow the female spectator to look and to identify in cinema –

a 'positive image' which then becomes inseparable from a self-respecting woman introduced by an implicit comparison with her opposite: the (female) spectator with no self-respect, a woman who needs to get some self-respect because, without it, she risks becoming whatever she looks at. But, paradoxically, the spectator who does identify with the degraded or inhuman images of cinema can only become what she already is insofar as no 'self-respecting person' could identify with these images in the first place. Thus what can sometimes appear as a feminist injunction against identification – an injunction which runs alongside a feminist interrogation of the difficulty of identification in cinema for women – seems to derive, on the one hand, from a loss of distinction between the spectator and the image on screen and, on the other hand, from an assimilation of the effects of cinema to a type of usurpation or (pre)occupation of the spectator.

That loss of distinction, and the displacement or, more strongly, the destruction of the spectator which accompanies it, is a central concern for what is, perhaps, the most famous denunciation of the culture industry. In *Dialectic of Enlightenment*, written while the authors were in exile in Hollywood and first published in 1944, Theodor Adorno and Max Horkheimer cast looking in the cinema as a form of dereliction with spectators unequivocally the victims of what they see: 'Real life is becoming indistinguishable from the movies . . . the film forces its victims to equate it directly with reality' (Adorno and Horkheimer 1979: 126). This remains one of their most serious charges against cinema – that the cinematic image reproduces and affirms 'things as they are' while the spectator becomes the mutilated realization of an industrialization of consciousness which reproduces capitalist relations of production by 'occupying men's senses' (ibid.: 131). That occupation, at the most intimate level of fantasy, destroys fantasy by making identification, as the wish to be like, impossible:

> Of course the starlet is meant to symbolize the typist in such a way that the splendid evening dress seems meant for the actress as distinct from the real girl. The girls in the audience not only feel that they could be on the screen, but realize the great gulf separating them from it. Only one girl can draw the lucky ticket, only one man can win the prize, and if, mathematically, all have the same chance, yet this is so infinitesimal for each one that he or she will do best to write it off and rejoice in the other's success, which might just as well have been his or hers, and somehow never

is. Whenever the culture industry still issues an invitation naively
to identify, it is immediately withdrawn. No one can escape from
himself any more. Once a member of the audience could see his
own wedding in the one shown in the film. Now the lucky actors
on the screen are copies of the same category as every member of
the public, but such equality only demonstrates the insurmount-
able separation of the human elements. The perfect similarity is
the absolute difference.

(ibid.: 145)

Rather than fantasmatic identification, rather than escapism, the
experience of cinema described in this passage familarizes a mass
spectator with the vagaries of chance against which there is no appeal
and before which no one is special, no one makes any difference.
There can be no identification, or no naive identification, because
there is too much recognition – when everyone is the same, identification with the images on the screen in the name of a desire to be like
them gives way before the realization that the image is standing in
for the spectator. Thus the girl's fantasy has no place beyond the
apparently paradoxical act of seeing the image in herself and then
recognizing its absolute difference before giving up the fantasy of
ever being like or ever being chosen. This is not a fetishistic way of
looking ('I know . . . but all the same') because there is no compensation, no escape, other than into a kind of altruism ('Rejoice in the
other's success'), into a form of social bonding which undoes fantasy,
bringing it, disappointed, into the service of social reality or social
resignation. That resignation becomes the catastrophe of the culture
industry for Adorno and Horkheimer because, as J.M. Bernstein has
recently pointed out, 'the question of the culture industry is raised
from the perspective of its relation to the possibilities for social
transformation' (Bernstein 1991: 2). The desire for transformation
informs both what looks like the sometimes violent exclusivity of a
modernist antagonism toward and differentiation of itself from 'the
mass' in Adorno and Horkheimer's critique of the culture industry
and the anxiety associated with the way in which that industry works
on and through fantasy and pleasure. What seems to be both equally
terrifying and sickening about the cinematic image is that it destroys
fantasy while at the same time securing pleasure. Just before their
description of identification in cinema, for example, Adorno and
Horkheimer assert the 'original affinity of business and amusement',
the task of amusement being to 'defend society':

To be pleased means to say Yes . . . Pleasure always means not to
think about anything, to forget suffering even where it is shown.
Basically it is helplessness. It is flight; not, as is asserted, flight
from a wretched reality, but from the last remaining thought of
resistance.

(Adorno and Horkheimer 1979: 144)

As an occupying force, then, cinema skews the spectator's relation
to pleasure, or, rather, makes pleasure the same as the death drive
insofar as that drive aims not at aggression but at an absence of
stimulation. Further, the charge that cinema turns pleasure into death
by mobilizing a conformist social fantasy cuts across any distinction between mass and avant-garde film – in 1944, Adorno and
Horkheimer make partial exceptions only of the grotesques and the
funnies – and puts the death drive on the side of a massified social
made secure against affect.

In 'The Schema of Mass Culture', Adorno makes this indistinction
between pleasure and death internal to the film process as such.
Images are 'seized' and frozen by cinema, put to a death that extracts
obedience from the spectators:

Through fixation the mask transforms what is utterly unthinglike,
expression itself, into horror over the fact that a human face can
be so arrested, and then transforms the horror into obedience
before the mortified face. That is the secret of the 'keep smiling'
attitude. The face becomes a dead letter by freezing the most living
thing about it, namely its laughter. The film fulfils the old
children's threat of the ugly grimace which freezes when the wind
changes or the clock strikes. And here it strikes the hour of total
domination. The masks of the film are so many emblems of
authority.

(Adorno 1991: 82)

This passage is an example both of the urgency and the difficulty
which characterizes Adorno's writing on cinema and of the way that
his attention to its aesthetic process is always bound up with a
question about cinema as industry, as institution and as social effect.
In fact, the move from the technique of cinema (the shot, the edit)
to its devastating, if not totalitarian, exercise of authority is made
remarkably quickly – so quickly and so insistently that it becomes
difficult to reconstruct the links between cinema and social on which
the argument depends. On the one hand, Adorno is concerned with

how cinema uses the image and with the transition from silent to sound films, a transition that he reads as both an expulsion of the dialectic between image and caption and a subsequent devaluation of the power of the image:

> In the older type of film images and written signs still alternated with one another and the antithesis of the two lent emphasis to the image-character of the images. But this dialectic like every other was unbearable to mass culture. It has expelled writing from the film as an alien presence but only to transform the images themselves completely into the writing which they have then absorbed in turn.
>
> (ibid.: 81)

On the other hand, as the last sentence of this passage indicates, Adorno is aiming, though he doesn't name it as such, at the narrative function of cinema, a function invested both in the sound-track and in the framing and sequencing of images: 'The images are seized but not contemplated. The film reel draws the eye along just like a line of writing and it turns the page with the gentle jolt of every scene change' (ibid.: 81).

Thus Adorno shifts between image and writing, image and narrative, image and sound, in an attempt to locate the deadly *authority* of cinema. Tentatively, the violent seizure of the image is bound up with the inevitable movement from frame to frame, a movement which paradoxically freezes the image by putting it beyond reflection or contemplation. In one sense, then, the image is transformed into writing because we can no longer look at it. This, Adorno insists, is the 'book-like character' of the film and it is in its 'writing' that he locates the 'secret doctrine' or message of capital:

> When a film presents us with a strikingly beautiful young woman it may officially approve or disapprove of her, she may be glorified as a successful heroine or punished as a vamp. Yet as a written character she announces something quite different from the psychological banners draped around her grinning mouth, namely the injunction to be like her.
>
> (ibid.: 81)

Intriguingly, the image of a woman that, as we shall see, puts Laura Mulvey on the track of a patriarchal unconscious, alerts Adorno to the presence of capitalist ideology for which the woman has become a mask, carrying the domination and authority of capital through cinema. But Adorno's distinction between the *image* of the 'strikingly beautiful woman', the film's official – narrative – approval or disapproval of her and her function as a 'written character' is confusing given his assertion of the relative failure of the 'image-character' of the image in the sound film. The image of the woman calls for a further differentiation between writing and narrative in relation to the cinematic image; that is, Adorno seems to be making a distinction between the 'writing' that is the film narrative – the movement of the film from one scene to another – and the writing somehow contained in the image itself. It is as if the written character of the image works beyond the narrative of the film insofar as the story told by the film about what happens to the woman doesn't matter. Heroine or vamp, what matters is the woman's physical and visible beauty because the spectacle of her beauty contains and carries the message of capital: 'be like'. That message transcends any narrative framing of the image taking place through the film text. In this sense, the image can retrieve its place as the privileged signifier of cinema. But this privilege is bought at the price of an assimilation of the cinematic image to the social structure of capital. Capital's message is written into the image and thus transforms cinema into the very type or model of its social process.

Because he reads cinema in terms of this overriding identification between image and capital, Adorno can describe the masks of film as so many 'emblems of authority' (ibid.: 82). This is a cinema occupied by a social which is itself more or less assimilable to the workings of capital. Thus the loss of any distinction between film and reality in Adorno and Horkheimer's analysis of the culture industry ('the film forces its victims to equate it directly with reality') has less to do with a fantasmatic invasion of the real associated with a culture saturated by the media, or the mediatization of the social, than with the pressure of reality on the 'dream factories' themselves. In this sense, a familiar account of mass culture as escapism or distraction – the account that, for example, runs through Hortense Powdermaker's cultural anthropology of the cinema as a kind of collective daydream providing 'wisely or unwisely [for] man's need for escape from his anxieties' (Powder-maker 1950: 15) – gives way before Adorno's critique of cinema as a type of social superego, commanding obedience from its spectators via the borrowed injunction: 'be like'. The demand for conformity and obedience issued by the culture industry destroys any claims it might make for itself as a necessary distraction from the exhaustion of everyday living, or what Adorno and Horkheimer deride as its 'function of diverting minds which it boasts about so loudly' (Adorno and Horkheimer 1979: 139). What is being proposed is a more unsettling account of distraction working in and through a cinema that 'murders' its spectators by forcing them into assimilating themselves with something dead, an assimilation which takes place through a participation in the translation of the images of cinema into its rhetoric of command:

> The viewer is required constantly to translate the images back into writing. The exercise of obedience inheres in the fact of translation itself as soon as it takes place automatically . . . [O]nce there they obey. They assimilate themselves to what is dead.
>
> (Adorno 1991: 81–2)

Twenty years later, in 'Transparencies on Film' published in 1966, Adorno explained the occupying and deadly force of cinema in terms which intimately associate a certain type of feminine beauty and a regressive paternal function. Almost conceding the possibility of a critical cinema associated with the *Oberhausen* group and the film theory and practice of his friend and associate, Alexander Kluge, he differentiated between the techniques and aesthetics of 'critical' and 'mass' film by making a distinction between two kinds of female beauty:

> While in autonomous art anything lagging behind the already established technical standard does not rate, *vis-à-vis* the culture industry – whose standard excludes everything but the pre-digested and the already integrated, just as the cosmetic trade eliminates facial wrinkles – works which have not completely mastered their technique, conveying as a result something con-solingly uncontrolled and accidental, have a liberating quality. In them the flaws of a pretty girl's complexion become the corrective to the immaculate face of the professional star.
>
> (Adorno 1991: 154)

This distinction is then mapped onto the generational polemics which characterized the clash between the *Oberhausen* group in their attempt to develop a 'New' German Cinema and the Hollywood film industry; that is, onto the difference between the so-called 'Kiddy's Cinema' and 'Daddy's Cinema' – the mass cultural 'trash' dismissed by Adorno for the immaturity of its experience 'acquired during the adolescence of the medium': 'What is repulsive about Daddy's

Cinema is its infantile character, regression manufactured on an industrial scale' (ibid.: 154).

The temporal contortion of Adorno's critique here describes a cinema that assumes a paternal function and then regresses – not just to adolescence but to an infantilism which is repulsive because it requires a debasement of that paternity, even its perversion, in the polymorphous sexuality characteristic of infancy. In other words, something about cinema seduces its spectators into a social identification which overwhelms them into resignation and conformity via the perversion of a paternal function which yet remains the 'model for collective behaviour' (ibid.: 158). In this context, it is worth noting that Andreas Huyssen has described the analysis of an objective decline in the authority of the father in the bourgeois family as one of the key tenets of the social and critical theory of the Frankfurt School. That decline, he suggests, was read as evidence of an increasing conformity to, and dependence on, external authority, a dependence which then disrupts the internalization of authority supposed to be a 'necessary prerequisite for the later (mature) rejection of authority by a strong ego' (Huyssen 1986: 22). In *Dialectic of Enlightenment*, for example, Adorno and Horkheimer were already suggesting that in our 'civilization of employees the dignity of the father (questionable anyhow) vanishes . . . [T]he Führer's gesticulations before the masses, or the suitor's before his sweetheart, assume specifically masochistic traits' (Adorno and Horkheimer 1979: 153). The description of a dependent ego structure, then, is clearly indissociable from the analysis of a mass capitulation to Nazism, to Hitler – a perverse type of substitute father. Crucially, as the passage from 'Transparencies on Film' suggests (and as Huyssen has also argued), the culture industry itself starts to be understood as a decisive element in the simultaneous degradation of the ego, the father and the social; the culture industry 'is seen as one of the major factors preventing . . . "healthy" internalization and replacing it by those external standards of behaviour which inevitably lead to conformism' (Huyssen 1986: 22).

In this sense, then, the recuperation of a sociality and a cinematic aesthetics understood to be more or less effectively ruined becomes the objective of the New German Cinema – Adorno's 'Kiddy's Cinema' – and of the oppositional film-making practice and the cultural and political theory associated with Alexander Kluge. 'Since 1933 we have been waging a war that has not stopped', Kluge has said in an interview with Stuart Liebman in 1988: 'National

Socialism is the problem, the problem of our youth, that Critical Theory worked on' (Liebman 1988: 45). Without attempting a comprehensive reading of Kluge's critical theory, I want to draw attention to his critique of mass or mainstream cinema as a cinema which disarticulates the spectator from his or her own 'interests' by dispossessing him or her of the capacity for (oppositional) fantasy. In the interview with Liebman, Kluge comments:

> I cannot really say that *Out of Africa* is not directed at escapism and *Rambo* clearly has little to do with real experience. Rather it is a stylization of the feelings of omnipotence of an eight-year-old . . . [it] shows the omnipotence of men. *Rambo* is a gruesome way of expressing fantasies of omnipotence. That is, so to speak, what the movies are . . . the cinema has slid down into 'kids' pictures'. I say this not as a critic but because one must understand this change.
>
> (ibid.: 26–7)

In a study of his critical and aesthetic theory, Miriam Hansen points to Kluge's condemnation of the 'two warring factions in German film production . . . the aesthetically unspeakable enterprises of commercial cinema – polemically dubbed Pornokultur and a Kunstfilmkultur struggling for economic existence as well as for an audience' (Hansen 1981–2: 37). Kluge proposed a cinema oriented to the productive force of the spectator, a cinema that both Porno- and Kunstkultur fall short of: 'It is the spectator who actually produces the film, as the film on screen sets in motion the film in the mind of the spectator' (ibid.: 39). But there is also something totalizing about Kluge's charge against contemporary mainstream cinema and it rests uneasily alongside his disarming 'I say this not as a critic'. The other side of Kluge's project for a critical cinema is a critique of both mainstream film and the mass spectator as above all, and I think suspiciously, readable:

> It is not only a political question, but a consequence of a persistent and total overburdening of people, which expresses itself ever farther from the sphere of their lives as producers. *They* suffer, they experience cognitive dissonance when *they perceive how they live*. If I feel myself as the producer of my life, then I am unhappy. So I would rather be a spectator of my life. I would rather change my life this way since I cannot change it in society. So at night I see films that are different from my experiences during the day. Thus there is a strict separation between experience and the

cinema. That is the obstacle for *our films*. For we are people of the
'60s and we do not believe in the opposition between experience
and fiction.

(Liebman 1988: 27; my italics)

The slide between pronouns here – from 'they' to 'I' to 'we' –
underlines the difficulty for Kluge of finding a place from which to
speak about a suffering that 'they' endure, with which 'I', via that
'if', can identify and that 'we', via a critical cinema, want to oppose.
'Our films' confront two problems: spectatorship as a strategy for
warding off misery and a form of cinematic fantasy mutilated by its
separation from reality, a separation which then marks the distinction
between the 'people' of the 1960s and the 1980s. The escapist or
omnipotent fantasy that Kluge ascribes to films as diverse as *Out of
Africa* and *Rambo* moves in as a response to a failure of the political
and cultural imagination. The separation between 'experience and
fiction', 'experience and cinema', is used to suggest that even the
'relation of dependency between fantasy and the experience of
alienated reality' has been disrupted (Negt and Kluge 1988: 76). For
Kluge, that disruption deprives fantasy of one of its essential
political functions as a form of inverted and critical consciousness
in relation to the real, a relation that a sufficiently critical practice
might grasp and expose. Thus what could be called the truth value
of fantasy is subject to two limitations in Kluge's analysis – though
it should be said that he is still using the category of escapist fantasy
to read off an account of collective impotence and alienation. First,
in a reading put forward with Oskar Negt in *The Public Sphere and
Experience* and excerpted in *October* in 1988, Kluge suggests that
its mode of production disrupts the dependent relation between
fantasy and experience. While 'by virtue of its mode of production,
fantasy represents an unconscious practical criticism of alienation',
it also tends to 'distance itself from the alienated labour process and
to translate itself into timeless and ahistorical modes of production'
(ibid.: 79). In other words, fantasy is provoked as a defence against
the external world and its flight from that world tends to transform
engaged critique into a form of destruction of the subject's ability to
represent reality; fantasy threatens to 'prevent the worker from
representing his interests in reality' by seducing him into an imaginary that does not, and cannot, exist (ibid.: 79).
    But this is not the decisive limitation because the turning away
from reality is overcome by a tendency for fantasies 'once they have

reached a certain distance from reality, to turn around and face up to real situations' (ibid.: 79). The pressure of the real prevails because the very success of fantasy – its diminution of what Kluge describes as the 'nightmarish quality' of alienated reality – turns it back to that reality. Fantasy holds or contains reality, fashions it in accordance with a logic of tolerability which comes back to those 'interests', at once so suspiciously obvious and so elusive, and to a question about what the worker wants. The second limitation on fantasy, and the real threat to its return to the real is the consciousness industry, exemplified by mainstream cinema:

> The existence of the subliminal activity of human consciousness – which, owing to its neglect hitherto by bourgeois interests and the public sphere, represents a partly autonomous mode of experience for the working class – is today threatened because it is precisely the workings of fantasy that constitute the raw material and the medium for the expansion of the consciousness industry.
>
> (ibid.: 77)

As Kluge sets up the relation between fantasy and cinema as a form of usurpation of the one by the other, it is as if the more we go to cinema, the less our fantasies can be our own. Crucially, that usurpation works through the regressive fantasies of omnipotence which Kluge associates with a historically new cinematic and political brutalism, exemplified by *Rambo*, supposed both to mobilize and satisfy a fantasy of masculinity and to exclude women from cinema. The female spectator is disidentified with what takes place on the screens of mainstream cinema not only, Kluge suggests, because women's fear of rape keeps them out of the public space of cinema but also because the films shown there are 'too coarse' for women: 'Why would they look at *Rambo* when they want their feelings to be treated gently? These are films for young men, not for women at all. The identifications do not work this way' (Liebman 1988: 29–30).

As soon as young men become the privileged objects of cinema, so masculinity becomes inseparable from a type of debasement and the young male spectator ends up on the side of the regression and illusion on which mainstream cinema is said to depend. But while Kluge starts to undermine an association between femininity and the masses which has persisted in social and cultural theory since the nineteenth century, he does so only by producing femininity as cliché – the cliché of women who want their feelings treated gently.[1] An alliance between the critical and the female spectator is thus bought at the price of a distinction which recalls Freud's differentiation – discussed in more detail in the next chapter – between 'ambitious' masculine and 'erotic' feminine fantasy: the corollary of a young and violent masculinity is the passive and gentle woman excluded from cinema and its fantasies of ambition and omnipotence.

So much at issue for feminist film theory over the last two decades, that gesture of exclusion has a history going back to the very origins of cinema. We can take the following from Emma Virginia Fish's *The Boy-Girl Adolescent Period*, first published in 1911, as a starting-point:

> While in most cities the law forbids the attendance of youths under 16 unchaperoned by an adult, this law is often not enforced, and already boys have been arrested for crimes of burglary, etc., which they have confessed have been suggested by these pictures in such attractive form as to lead them to try their hands at picking locks, robbing safes, and even robbing trains. Recently, in one of our large cities, little girls, arrested for improper conduct, confessed to police authorities that under cover of the semi-darkness in the moving picture theatres men have said vile things to them and have attempted insults. It is a burning shame that an amusement with such immense possibilities for good as the kinetograph should be put to such vile uses.
>
> (Fish 1911, cited in Doherty 1988: 116)

Fish seems to anticipate here what will become two essential elements in the response to cinema and spectatorship. Pointing to the 'immense possibilities' of the moving picture, Fish expresses the desire to harness its productive potential which can be seen at work, for example, in the Motion Picture Production Code established in the United States during the 1930s. 'Correct' entertainment, for that code, 'raise[d] the standards of the whole nation', it aimed to 'recreate and rebuild human beings exhausted with the realities of living' (Powdermaker 1950: 57). But, and via a familiar link between immaturity, suggestibility and 'the masses', it is precisely the popular appeal of cinema which can so easily transform it into a social threat. Thus according to the British Board of Film Censors, set up in 1913, a 'not inconsiderable proportion' of the cinema-going public exhibited 'immature judgement' (Porter 1985: 94). On the one hand, then, Fish is concerned with cinema as a mass cultural phenomenon and as an instrument of mass influence. On the other hand, at the same time as she voices a sense that, unless controlled, cinema seduces its spectators into deviance, she also makes a distinction between the boys who imitate what takes place on the screen and the girls who are subjected to a sexual assault in the public space of cinema. The girl imitates and takes outside the 'improper conduct' learned in the cinema, certainly, but her relation to the screen remains elusive. The boys are copying what they have seen but the link between what the girl was looking at and the insulting sexual attention she receives is unclear. In fact, there is nothing to say that she was looking at all. Seclusion and semi-darkness govern what happens to her in the cinema and not the images of robbing safes and picking locks that fascinate and possibly motivate the boys.

When she makes this distinction between boys who identify with and act out the images and narratives on screen and girls who become, in one sense, the sexual victims of cinema, Fish seems to rehearse the sexual differentiation of spectatorship which has been so central to feminist film theory since the 1970s. Laura Mulvey set the terms of a debate which has haunted feminist film theory since the publication of 'Visual Pleasure and Narrative Cinema' in 1975: 'Woman as Image, Man as Bearer of the Look . . . The determining male gaze projects its phantasy on to the female figure which is styled accordingly'; 'Recent writing in *Screen* about psychoanalysis and the cinema has not sufficiently brought out the importance of the representation of the female form in a symbolic order in which, in the last resort, it speaks castration and nothing else' (Mulvey 1975: 27; 22). These are the terms of what Miriam Hansen has described as the 'classical choreography of the look' in feminist film theory (Hansen 1986: 11). The woman becomes the object of a male look which has to defend itself, voyeuristically or fetishistically, against the threat inherent in the image of the 'castrated' woman. Further, the male look finds a way to identify – more or less pleasurably, more or less omnipotently – with its like on screen:

> As the spectator identifies with the main male protagonist, he projects his look on to that of his like, his screen surrogate, so that the power of the male protagonist as he controls events coincides with the active power of the erotic look, both giving a satisfying sense of omnipotence.
>
> (Mulvey 1975: 28)

By contrast, the female spectator has no choice but to witness her 'stolen' image, sexualized and implicitly degraded in the name of a

cinema made over to the male spectator: 'In their traditional exhib-
itionist role women are simultaneously looked at and displayed, with
their appearance coded for strong visual and erotic impact so that
they can be said to connote to-be-looked-at-ness' (ibid.: 27).

Mulvey has commented on the way that her early paper took on
'a life of its own' (Mulvey 1989: vii) in feminist and psychoanalytic
film theory, a life that Janet Bergstrom and Mary Ann Doane confirm
in their introduction to 'The Spectatrix' – the special issue of
Camera Obscura published in 1989 and devoted to the 'problem' of
the female spectator. Including four surveys and over fifty individual
responses to a questionnaire drafted by Bergstrom and Doane, 'The
Spectatrix' is itself a monument to the elusive and yet 'overly
familiar' figure of the female spectator which has so frequently
dominated feminist analyses of spectatorship and cinema (Bergstrom
and Doane 1989: 13). Bergstrom and Doane situate Mulvey's 'Visual
Pleasure' as both a founding moment for feminist and psychoanalytic theories of spectatorship and as a moment of compulsion for
feminist film theory after which it becomes almost impossible to
think about looking in cinema outside of the concepts of fetishism,
voyeurism and castration – outside, that is, of sexual difference:

> It was as though her essay produced a stunning recognition-effect
> which thereafter determined the terms of discussion . . . For a
> while it seemed (and often still seems) that every feminist writing
> on film felt compelled to situate herself in relation to Mulvey's
> essay . . . If we insist upon situating Mulvey's essay as the
> inaugural moment – the condition of possibility – of an extended
> theorization of the female spectator, it must also be remembered
> that this 'origin' is constituted by an absence. In 'Visual Pleasure,'
> there is no trace of the female spectator. Indeed, spectatorship is
> incontrovertibly masculine, as evidenced by the frequently noted
> pronoun 'he' in the essay. What was so overwhelmingly recogniz-
> able in 'Visual Pleasure' was our own absence. Thus, one of the
> questions raised about Mulvey's psychoanalytic framework was
> inevitably, 'What about the female spectator?'
>
> (ibid.: 7)

Thus Mulvey's drastic sexing of the look as masculine allowed
feminist film theory to recognize itself in a structure of spectatorship
that worked through the absence or exclusion of the woman, an
absence which generates what, in her own contribution to 'The
Spectatrix', Mulvey calls the 'dilemma of the female spectator'. 'I

became aware of the "female spectator" first as a dilemma within myself', Mulvey acknowledges, and then goes on to derive that dilemma from the 'influence of the Women's Movement' (Mulvey 1989: 248). Feminism intervened in a love for Hollywood which had been, for her, 'more or less without question' and breached the gap between mass entertainment and a high cultural aesthetic:

> [T]hey [Hollywood films] introduced me to a visual language of popular, mass entertainment, an aesthetic that was not acknowledged by the traditions of British high culture within which I grew up. Then feminism intervened, like an insistent tug at one's sleeve, breaking the spell by drawing attention to the problems posed by the images of women on the screen, so that sometimes films that had previously thrilled me or moved me to tears simply turned into irritants before my eyes.
>
> (ibid.)

We can read a history of two decades of the Women's Movement embedded in Mulvey's statement and its powerful personification of a feminism that moved in on, and then took up its place in, what Freud describes as our most secret, intimate and cherished possessions – our fantasies and daydreams (*PFL* 10: 133). In the transformation of something it would probably be too easy to call pleasure, we can trace the logic of both the headline to the second section of 'Visual Pleasure' – 'Destruction of Pleasure as a Radical Weapon' – and Mulvey's announcement of her political intention: 'It is said that analysing pleasure, or beauty, destroys it. That is the intention of this article' (Mulvey 1975: 24). This radical mistrust of pleasure signals an over-determined moment of anxiety, of loss and of desire for something else in feminist theory and practice, a moment that Mulvey can only start to address by investing in the 'passionate detachment' of an oppositional or avant-garde filmmaking practice which owes so much to a Brechtian aesthetics:

> The first blow against the monolithic accumulation of traditional film conventions (already undertaken by radical filmmakers) is to free the look of the camera into its materiality in time and space and the look of the audience into dialectics, passionate detachment.
>
> (ibid.: 33)

Such a radical aesthetics, in Mulvey's view, works against the objectifying voyeurism and the self-aggrandizing identifications of mainstream cinema and towards what, in 'The Spectatrix', she

...s transition entailed others, for instance: from consumption to criticism, from criticism to filmmaking; a transition from excitement with the images of popular cinema to excitement with the critical languages of semiotics and psychoanalysis that simultaneously enhanced and unmasked those images.

(ibid.)

This fascination with fascination helps to explain why Mulvey's work has mesmerized feminist film theory. Certainly, the turn to feminism and to psychoanalysis starts to look like a transference of fascination, of preoccupation, and a compensation for whatever it is that has been lost. Mulvey is explicit: '[P]sychoanalytic theory offered something besides an appropriate critical vocabulary and an analytic tool; it offered a new and different kind of pleasure that compensated, in a way, for the sense of loss' (ibid.). Thus feminism and psychoanalysis became tools in an absorbing act of decipherment for Mulvey's film theory and for its discovery of a form of 'active spectatorship' which aimed to lay bare the 'social unconscious under patriarchy' (ibid.). Further, her interrogation of fascination defines Mulvey's politically oppositional appropriation of psychoanalysis. 'This paper', she explains at the beginning of 'Visual Pleasure', 'intends to use psychoanalysis to discover where and how the fascination of film is reinforced by pre-existing patterns of fascination already at work within the individual subject and the social formations that have moulded him' (Mulvey 1975: 22).

Insofar as those formations are dependent on 'an idea of woman' as lack (ibid.), sexual difference becomes an essential category in Mulvey's analysis – an analysis which seems, at times, to be on an edge between a Marxist or materialist reading of cinema and more feminist and psychoanalytic approaches to film. At the juncture between a Marxist – or, more specifically, Althusserian – theory of ideological interpellation of the subject into the social and a feminist critique of patriarchal and masculine forms of fantasy in the cinema, Mulvey starts to formulate the relation between cinematic representation, social identification and sexual difference. At the same time, the functionalism inherent in Mulvey's profile of a subject-spectator slotted into place by the social formations that have moulded him has, perhaps, contributed to the virtual eclipse of that aspect of her critique in feminist appropriations of her work. Mulvey's subject-spectator is *realized* by pre-existing social structures in a way that sits uneasily alongside her use of a psychoanalysis for which identity is a process that is, as Jacqueline Rose explains it, 'neither simply achieved nor ever complete' (Rose 1986: 7). As Joan Copjec has pointed out in a recent critique of the subject of film theory, a conception of a subject realized through recognition of its visible image loses sight of a specifically psychoanalytic account of subjectivity. In 'The Orthopsychic Subject: Film Theory and the Reception of Lacan', published in *October* in 1989, Copjec rereads Lacan's theory of the gaze in an attempt to shift what she describes as the

> central misconception of film theory: believing itself to be follow-
> ing Lacan, it conceives the screen as mirror; in doing so, however,
> it operates in ignorance of, and at the expense of, Lacan's more
> radical insight, whereby the mirror is conceived as screen.
>
> (Copjec 1989: 54)

Copjec traces that misconception through the development of film theory in the 1970s, citing the work of Jean-Louis Baudry, Christian Metz and Jean-Louis Comolli, and the film journal *Screen*, as instrumental in a privileging of Lacan's concept of the imaginary in the analysis of cinema. Copjec acknowledges that the description of cinema as an apparatus (or *dispositif*, a term borrowed, she points out, from Gaston Bachelard) was part of an attempt to account for the specificity of the cinematic institution: the 'reality effect' of the film image which is also uniquely absent; the constitution of the subject as spectator; the production of pleasure that is, in turn, essential to the reproduction of cinema as an 'ideological state apparatus'. Thus Lacan's theory of the mirror stage has been used to support a description of cinema as a source of regressive and hallucinatory satisfaction for a spectator-subject who identifies with his or her own act of perception via a primary identification with the camera. That description, and its subject, conceives the screen as mirror and the spectator as, in Constance Penley's terms, 'centred for absolute mastery over the visual domain' (Penley 1989: 63). That mastery then allows the subject-spectator to accept the images on screen as his 'own', or, as Copjec puts it, to become 'master of the image': 'The "reality effect" and the "subject effect" both name the same constructed impression: that the image makes the subject fully visible to itself' (Copjec 1989: 59).

 As Copjec goes on to show, film theory has consistently described both the reality and the subject effects of cinema as ideological in the sense that cinema works to produce a subject which, like the infant of the mirror stage, misrecognizes itself as coherent, as the self-identified 'source and centre of the represented world' (ibid.: 67). But despite the error implied by the very notion of misrecognition, the process through which the subject performs that error seems never to fail and it is this lack of failure – or rather, film theory's apparent attachment to this lack of failure – that Copjec starts to question by making a distinction between the Lacanian and the Foucauldian theories of the gaze. There is a tendency, she suggests, to collapse Lacan into Foucault insofar as film theory works with the *panoptic gaze* and with a subject that is the *realization* of its power. In effect, this amounts to the loss of the Lacanian theory of the subject as only ever the *effect* of a gaze. Copjec summarizes a 'Foucauldian' account of a subject made visible and knowable to itself via its identification with the objective surveillance of the institution as a subject determinate in the last instance through the clash of different identities or positions which are nevertheless *produced*. She then compares this version of the subject to Bachelard's orthopsychic subject of concealment. The orthopsychic relation, she suggests, unlike the panoptic one, assumes that the process of objective survey or surveillance allows thought to become *secret* or to remain *hidden*, 'even under the most intense scrutiny' – not because there is an 'original, private self that happens to find in objectivity a means (among others) of concealing itself' but because the very act of surveillance supposed to make the subject visible in fact makes it clear that 'the subject is external to itself, exists in a relation of "extimacy" (Lacan's word) with itself'. Further, both surveillance and extimacy cause the subject to 'appear to itself as culpable, as guilty of hiding something'. Thus: 'The objective relation to the self, Bachelard informs us, necessarily raises the insidious question that Nietzsche formulated thus: "To everything which man allows to become visible, one is thus able to demand: what does he wish to hide?"' (ibid.: 65).

This, however, is still not Lacan's theory of the gaze. Copjec draws another distinction between Bachelard and Lacan. Bachelard offers the subject a reprieve not in the full visibility of its image but in the 'process of *scrutinising* this image' so that scrutiny, or the quest for (self) knowledge, becomes a source of potential salvation for the subject of concealment. By contrast, Lacan detects *culpability* in the screening-off of the subject so that the Lacanian gaze signals neither visibility nor scrutiny but *guilt*: 'The gaze stands watch over the inculpation – the faulting and splitting – of the subject by the apparatus' (ibid.: 65). Not a visible subject of the gaze, then, but a guilty one; or, more precisely, a subject guilty in its very visibility because – and decisively – there is a type of secrecy internal to visibility, to looking as such, which disturbs any adequation between spectator and image and, with it, the metaphorization of the screen as a mirror. The mirror, Copjec insists, *assumes the function of a screen* not only because we inevitably disbelieve what we see but because that disbelief signals a suspicion – what is being concealed from me? – which turns visibility into a lure:

> This point at which something appears to be invisible, this point at which something seems to be missing from representation, some meaning left unrevealed, is the point of the Lacanian gaze . . . The image, the visual field, then takes on a terrifying alterity that prohibits the subject from seeing itself in the representation.
>
> (ibid.: 69)

It is this alterity of the image which disrupts what Copjec glosses as the ideological work of cinema – the production of the subject as coherence, as appropriative self-presence. If we follow her reading of Lacan's theory of the gaze, the subject

> comes into existence . . . through a desire which is still considered to be the *effect* of the law, but not its *realization* . . . [I]t is, rather, occasioned by impossibility, the impossibility of the subject's ever co-inciding with the real being from which representation cuts it off.
>
> (ibid.: 70)

In other words, Copjec's examination of the relation between guilt and vision in terms of a 'left-over' which forever escapes representation locates a specifically symbolic function of cinema against the stress on imaginary identification more usually associated with psychoanalytic approaches to film. At the same time, her displacement of the primacy of visibility in cinema is, in effect, a critique of a tendency in film theory to equate identification with (narcissistic) recognition of the self in the image on the screen. That equation, in turn, seems to come out of a distinction between the scopophilic look at an erotic object and the recognition that is the narcissistic aspect of the scopophilic drive – a distinction which is, I want to suggest, essential both to Mulvey's exemplary sexing of the look and to the residual functionalism which resists her psychoanalytic framework:

> Thus in film terms, one implies a separation of the erotic identity

of the subject from the object on the screen (active scopophilia), the other demands identification of the ego with the object on the screen through the spectator's fascination with and recognition of his like.

(Mulvey 1975: 26)

Insofar as film theory has equated identification with recognition, it has been caught up in the attempt to theorize the relation between an individual spectator and the screen, oscillating between the debased place of the feminine object and the illusory, or delusory, mastery of the masculine ideal ego. By separating scopophilia from identification through a distinction between the spectator's erotic identity secured in relation to an object and 'his' recognition of self in his like, Mulvey assumes that identification and object choice can be kept apart; whereas for a certain psychoanalytic reading – and I will come back to this – identification is the term which disturbs the very notion of an identity in place and, with it, the distinction between subject and object, between individual and collective, between what 'I' look at and what 'I' am. At this point, we need to go back to the Introduction to 'The Spectatrix' and, specifically, to Bergstrom and Doane's suggestion that Mulvey's radical project of destruction – and reconstruction – of the femininity and the pleasure constituted by the mass and masculine imaginary sketched out in 'Visual Pleasure' is inseparable from a certain malaise, from 'a kind of ennui' haunting feminist film theory which the authors link directly to Mulvey's use of psychoanalysis: '[O]ne of the questions raised about Mulvey's psychoanalytic framework was inevitably, "What about the female spectator?"' (Bergstrom and Doane 1989: 15; 7). Through this question, Bergstrom and Doane give expression to a sense that psychoanalysis cannot contain the dilemmas of the female spectator. As a number of the contributions to 'The Spectatrix' make clear, that sense is part of a more general unease with a psychoanalytic framework that has been so productive for film theory – not least because it has provided the terms for a theorization of looking as always something more than perception, as always saturated with desire – but which is felt to have become a restriction, legitimizing an ahistorical and abstract approach to spectatorship in which everything falls back onto sexuality and sexual difference. Ellen Seiter makes the point forcefully when she suggests that feminist engagement with female spectatorship through psycho-analysis is at a dead end:

I think that psychoanalytic theory has blinded feminist film studies to the significance of race and class difference. This is why theoretical work on the female spectator may have reached a dead end, while cultural studies (aspiring at its best to merge Marxism and feminism) has been marked by an enthusiasm for empirical work.

(Seiter 1989: 283–4)

Constance Penley may have this emphasis in mind when she refers to an 'unfortunate tendency in the newer research on women and popular culture to dismiss the work on subjectivity and sexual difference developed over the last fifteen years in feminist film theory' (Penley 1989b: 257). Certainly – and recalling Elizabeth Abel's summary of feminist suspicions of psychoanalysis discussed in Chapter 1 – a version of psychoanalysis as a lure which has 'blinded' feminist film studies to the importance of any difference other than the sexual runs through 'The Spectatrix'. Annette Kuhn formulates the problem as one of the 'relationship between subjectivity and social formation, and how to conceptualize femaleness/ femininity within the subject/social formation', concluding that: 'In the context of the "female spectator," the question is reduced to the connection between femininity as a mode of subjectivity and women as social beings' (Kuhn 1989: 214). Put this way, it seems that the female spectator has become the primary focus within film theory for the difficulty of trying to articulate sexual difference and social identification – or, to risk another over-familiar couple, psychoanalysis and Marxism. It is as if, in its possibly mournful turn to psychoanalysis, film theory loses or discards something which then keeps coming back in the guise of the 'social', of 'history', 'class', 'race', the 'real woman in the audience'. To put this slightly differently, the dominance of a psychoanalytic framework in feminist film theory seems to have restricted the problem of the female spectator to the difficulty of her femininity – a femininity which is then isolated from any other type of social identity or identification by the compelling blind spots of what Judith Mayne has recently described, in *Cinema and Spectatorship*, as the psychoanalytic 'master narrative':

How many times does one need to be told that individual film *x*, or film genre *y*, articulates the law of the father, assigns the spectator a position of male oedipal desire, marshals castration anxiety in the form of voyeurism and fetishism, before psycho-

analysis begins to sound less like the exploration of the unconscious, and more like a master plot?

(Mayne 1993: 68–9)

The impatience with psychoanalytic film criticism in this passage is
obvious and it goes hand in hand with the suggestion that there may
be an incompatibility between psychoanalysis and more 'social' or
'historical' readings of film. But Mayne also picks up on the
possibility that psychoanalytic film theory has, at times, forgotten its
psychoanalysis, forgotten the specificity of its objects – namely, the
categories of fantasy and the unconscious which would resist the
totalizing effects of the 'master plot'. Crucially, though, feminist
film theory does not always forget. In 'Feminism, Film Theory, and
the Bachelor Machines', first published in 1985, Constance Penley
invests a psychoanalytic theory of fantasy with precisely this
potential for 'dismantling the bachelor machines of film theory'
which represent cinema as a closed and self-sufficient system
working on and through the pleasurable captivation of its spectators
and the resolution of Oedipal desire. The influence of these 'bachelor
machines' makes itself felt in film theory, Penley suggests, both in
analyses of cinema as a 'technological, institutional, and psychical
"machine"' and in the theory of classical film narrative as itself a
machine, 'infinitely sustaining' and repeating the drama of Oedipal
conflict and the reduction of sexual difference to, in Raymond
Bellour's terms, 'a narcissistic doubling of the masculine subject'
(Penley 1989a: 58). Like Copjec, Penley acknowledges Baudry and
Metz's important stress on the specificity of cinema as an institution
– a stress which, once again, owes something to the influence of
Althusser's theory of ideology and subject interpellation set out in
his famous essay, 'Ideology and the Ideological State Apparatuses'
(1971). But she also criticizes the ahistorical and universal model of
the psyche which emerges through their work and, more precisely,
a pervasive assumption that 'the success of the apparatus in its
production of cinematic pleasure is due to the fact that it was, after
all, "built" in conformity to strictly wishfulfilling requirements'
(ibid.: 61). Here Penley voices a more general feminist discontent
with a tendency to lose sight of the fact that the supposed gratifications of the cinematic apparatus – scopophilia, fetishism, narcissism
– depend on a structure of sexual difference that has a price for the
woman.[2] A psychoanalytic account of fantasy, she insists, must
emphasize the sexualization of the drives through fantasy and the

distribution of sexual difference in and through the process of fantasy. At the same time, and above all, psychoanalysis has made the concepts of pleasure and fantasy irreducibly *difficult*:

> Surely psychoanalytic theory has offered us a more complex account of the vicissitudes of desire (the repetition compulsion and the death drive), let alone posited the desire for an unsatisfied desire (hysteria as the desire not to have one's desire satisfied). The question of pleasure has been a crucially troubling one for feminist film theory and filmmaking, and the theory of the apparatus appears to answer the question before it is even raised.
>
> (ibid.: 62)

Drawing on Laplanche and Pontalis's influential discussion of the staging and imaging of the subject and its desire in fantasy, in 'Fantasy and the Origins of Sexuality', Penley underlines the necessity for film analysis to present a

> more accurate description of the spectator's shifting and multiple identifications and a more comprehensive account of these same movements within the film: the perpetually changing configurations of the characters, for example, are a formal response to the unfolding of a fantasy that is the filmic fiction itself.
>
> (ibid.: 80)

The purchase, and the difficulty, of this more nuanced approach to cinematic fantasy is spelled out in Penley's contribution to 'The Spectatrix':

> I became convinced that, if we were going to look for a sexually differentiated spectator, we would have to look elsewhere than the unconscious – in modes of address or more conscious levels of fantasy, for example. In other words, sexual difference, one's unconscious sexual position, is constructed through the unconscious, but the unconscious is not itself sexually differentiated.
>
> (Penley 1989b: 256–7)

This emphasis on the unconscious does not lend itself easily to a psychoanalytic master narrative which can only ever find, and refind, the dramas of Oedipal conflict. Further, by refusing to forget the question of *address*, Penley resists a model of fantasy as absolute fluidity or instability, as 'anything goes'. On the contrary, Penley's stress on the mobility of the spectator's identifications across sexual difference coexists with an attention to cinema as a site and source of both fascination and of the articulation of the spectator with his or her own sex – the articulation which was so central to Mulvey's project. That project is still there and still agitating through what could be described as a theoretical wish that 'in this light, all films, and not just the products of Hollywood, would be seen and studied in their fully historical and social variety as dream factories' (Penley 1989a: 80).

There is, I think, the potential for an interminable, and possibly inevitable, oscillation built into the double demand made on psychoanalysis at this point – or, at least, on (one of) its accounts of fantasy *as* identification. What film theory seems to need from psychoanalysis is a theory of identification which can account for cinema as a site of both fantasmatic mobility and ideological fixation, of both individual 'desubjectivization' through the loss or failure of identity in fantasy and identification which goes beyond conscious recognition of whatever is being shown on screen. On the one hand, this double demand recalls a moment of repudiation of the concept of identification from within a film theory which situates itself as both Marxist and political. In 'Parenthesis or Indirect Route: An Attempt at a Theoretical Definition of the Relationship between Cinema and Politics', published in *Screen* in 1971, Jean-Paul Fargier dismisses the concept of identification as 'too psychological', distinguishing between the bourgeois spectator who recognizes himself on the screen and the working-class spectator who is mystified by what he sees. 'Two precise phenomena', Fargier suggests, 'throw light on the relationship cinema/politics at the juncture ideology/ politics':

The first is that of RECOGNITION. The audience recognise themselves on the screen: characters, ideas, myths, stories, structures, way of life. Here, much more than the concept of *identification* (which is too psychological) it is the concept of recognition which is at work . . . But to another section of the public, the mirror 'tells lies'. We have a class society dominated by the bourgeoisie, in which the cinema claims to be the same for everybody. However, a section of the cinema-going public consists of exploited workers, and in their case a second (but concomitant) ideological phenomenon occurs: MYSTIFICATION. They identify with what happens on the screen (mechanically) but they *cannot*, or ought not to be able to, recognise themselves in it.

(Fargier 1971: 137)

We can, perhaps, glimpse the traces of a self-respecting female spectator in this passage in the form of the working-class spectator who *ought not* to recognize himself on the screen – an injunction which exemplifies what seems to be a type of theoretical and moral opposition between the analysis of a group subject and con-figurations of social power and a psychological (or psychoanalytic) 'privileging' of the individual. In the name of a political difference between the workers and the bourgeoisie – and, I think, of a political cinema, an aesthetics of cinema that would be, in some sense, for the working class – Fargier, not unlike Mulvey, wants to displace both the concept and the process of identification as such. Working beyond recognition, identification is the very process through which the spectator is mystified because, it seems, identi-fication cannot fail to occur even if what the spectator is shown is someone else's life, someone else's image, someone else's fantasy. Mechanically, compulsively, the working-class spectator sees him-self where he is not, and cannot be; he may, if Kluge is right, seek out precisely those films which 'are different from my experiences during the day' because he would prefer to change his life via the screen than in the real world (Liebman 1988: 27). Thus, once again, the working-class spectator – who may be both indissociable and separable from the 'mass' spectators described by the Frankfurt School – becomes the victim of a cinema that belongs, in the final analysis, to capital.

On the other hand, Fargier's reading of identification as a more or less compulsive action which confounds identity across class recalls both recent feminist accounts of the female spectator who is simultaneously inside and outside of the fantasies of cinema and, to go back to what I suggested earlier might be specific to a psycho-analytic theory of its effects, identification as that which disturbs the very distinction between what I *look at* and what I *am*. It would be, I think – and 'The Spectatrix' confirms it – impossible to do justice to the range and complexity of the debates within feminist film theory on the problem of the female spectator. Jackie Stacey has, bravely, summarized the 'three rather frustrating options of mascul-inisation, masochism or marginality' which have been allocated to the female spectator in feminist film theory: she can look 'as a man'; she can identify with her objectification and alienation in the image; or, finally, she can take on, and, perhaps, rejoice in, her position outside, on the margins of, patriarchal fantasy (Stacey 1987: 51). What she cannot do, it seems, is to look and identify 'as a woman' –

though what it might mean to do this is a problem that goes far beyond feminist film theory. In her commentary on David Lynch's controversial *Blue Velvet*, for example, Barbara Creed describes a female spectator who identifies with what she sees on screen despite the fact that the images and narratives on display are not her 'own':

> For the present, this is a problem that the female spectator must confront. Despite being able to identify with the multiplicity of subject positions, for her the fictional characters of mainstream, male-centred cinema are not 'real beings, possessing life and action' because, in general, they belong to someone else's fantasy.
>
> (Creed 1988: 116)

Even if what the spectator is shown is 'someone else's fantasy', then, he or she is always able to identify; or, whether mass or masculine, the cinema is always able to dispossess its spectators via the alienated, and, I would add, preoccupying, identifications it solicits.

As Mary Ann Doane points out in her discussion of the 'woman's film', this sense of the female spectator – both within cinema and film theory – as 'stranded between incommensurable entities' is the inevitable result of the contradictions 'active at the level of the social/ psychological construction of female spectatorship' (Doane 1987: 7). To put this another way: the female spectator seems to carry a certain distress for feminist film theory, a distress which makes itself felt in the idea of a woman at once overwhelmed by and dissociated from cinematic fantasy. Tania Modleski, for example, has recast the female spectator as the daughter of a cinematic family romance. In 'Three Men and Baby M', published in the 'Male Trouble' issue of *Camera Obscura* in 1988, Modleski argues that a paternity that knows how to love has become something of a preoccupation for both cinema, in films like *Three Men and a Baby* (Leonard Nimoy 1987), and for television, in series like *Full House*, about 'three men and three little girls', and *My Two Dads* (Modleski 1988: 80). Noting that the female audience for these films are 'as amused and deeply touched . . . as men are – probably more so' (ibid.: 79–80), Modleski concludes her essay with a warning. It is not that cinema is engaged in a 'historically unprecedented, feminist-inspired, and altogether contemporary reconceptualization of the paternal role' (ibid.: 69). On the contrary:

> The fact that in every one of these cases the children reared exclusively by men are female suggests that the daughters are

being seduced *away* from feminism and into a world where they may become so 'dazzled' by the proliferating varieties of paternity that they are unable to see whose interests are really being served.
(ibid.: 80)

Modleski's specific reference in this passage is to the figure of the imaginary father theorized by Julia Kristeva in *Tales of Love* (1987) – a figure through whom Kristeva criticizes a tendency to describe a so-called contemporary social and political malaise as the effect of a decline in paternal authority. Christopher Lasch, discussed more fully in the next chapter, has, for example, made an appeal to a more authoritarian paternal structure in his lament for the social superego represented by 'fathers, teachers and preachers' (Lasch 1980: 11). And Janine Chasseguet-Smirgel gives an account of 'ideological' group identity organized around the 'mother of the pervert' and the refusal to recognize the law of the father (Chasseguet-Smirgel 1985: 12). Against this, Kristeva insists that there has been 'too much stress on the crisis in paternity as cause of psychotic discontent': 'Beyond the often fierce but artificial and incredible tyranny of the Law and the superego, the crisis in the paternal function that led to a deficiency of psychic space is in fact an erosion of the loving father' (Kristeva 1987: 378).

In Kristeva's reading, the loving father introduces a break on the fusion between mother and child. He saves the child from an abjection – very schematically, an auto-erotic submersion which blocks any recognition of the difference between infant and mother – that, left unchecked, would cut the infant off both from love and from the social. But, and crucially, the loving father can also be said to represent, or to work as, a *distraction*. That distraction is essential because it stands for what the mother desires beyond the infant: 'The imaginary father would thus be the indication that the mother is not complete but that she wants . . . Who? What? . . . "At any rate, not I"' (ibid.: 41). But, again, and precisely as distraction, the figure of the loving father is profoundly ambivalent, his love able to cut both ways. What is there, after all, to prevent the imaginary father from becoming not just proof of the mother's desire beyond her child – a proof which releases the child into the world – but also the object that 'dazzles' or (pre)occupies the child, which presents itself as the only object the child can want? When we ask this question it immediately matters that Kristeva's imaginary father is still a paternal function and that distraction is being symbolized by a paternity which can always become – perhaps whether it wants to or not – either seductive or perverse. In fact, Kristeva puts the question 'seducer or ideal father' (ibid.: 46) to her imaginary construct, a question that Modleski's reading of *Three Men and a Baby* answers by invoking the father-as-pervert:

> This Peter Pan fantasy (*about* a man named Peter, and brought to us by Walt Disney) even incorporates a kind of Wendy figure at the end, a woman who is not (or not any longer) the object of any man's desire but part of the group which gets to play perpetually with the baby.
>
> (Modleski 1988: 75)

Modleski is here picking up on what she sees as an important trend in 1980s cinema – a cinema which presents us with a version of family life that can be simultaneously seductive and repellent. For Modleski, the sexual politics of the representation of paternity in the 1980s have to be viewed in the context both of a feminist demand that men take on more responsibility for parenting and of the legal and ethical issues, in particular the rights of fathers, raised by the possibility of surrogate mothers. In particular, she draws attention to the priority given to the father–daughter relation in *Three Men and a Baby*, a priority through which the adult woman is marginalized both as object of desire and as a mother. The film's status as a sentimental comedy, she suggests, sustains its representation of a paedophilic desire to 'freeze the life process so that the object will not outgrow the desire' while the fathers 'refuse to grow up' (ibid.). This infantilization of culture is then matched by a sexualization of the infantile which allows what Modleski describes as 'some shockingly voyeuristic shots . . . of the baby's genitals' and a film 'laden with jokes about a female baby as an adequate object of sexual desire for three aging bachelors (for example, when Jack takes a shower with her)' (ibid.: 72; 71). Given feminist attention to the prevalence of the sexual abuse of children, the image of a baby presented as an 'adequate object of desire' to a man is bound to raise the question of the relation between cinematic representation and the social for film theory. But what struck me about Modleski's reading was her sense that the perversity of this cinema was aimed not only at the daughters inside the narratives of loving fathers, of fathers loving daughters, but also at the daughters outside looking on. In this sense, the female spectator is reconstituted as a woman seduced away from feminism into a self-violating identification with the father, as the daughter of a seductive paternity working within and beyond cinema.

Recalling Adorno's recourse to a paternal metaphor to describe the debased functioning of cinema, there is an unsettling logic to this cinematic father who, when he 'loves', presents us with a cinema which assumes paternity through a perversity that goes far beyond the objectifying voyeurism and fetishism central to the classic feminist theory of spectatorship. Something else is at issue here, something other than narcissistic recognition of self, or scopophilic objectification of the other, on screen. Though differently, both Adorno and Modleski point to the need for an account of spectatorship as the effect of a dispossessing or distracted identification with a cinema made over to the father's interest and the father's desire – as the effect, then, of a more or less disturbing relation to a paternal instance. Suspending the question of identification with the father's desire for the moment, a passage from Freud's *The Interpretation of Dreams* can be used to elaborate on the dispossession which seems to put the critique of mass culture into dialogue with a feminist analysis of female spectatorship. 'It is my experience', Freud writes, 'and one to which I have found no exception, that every dream deals with the dreamer himself' (*PFL* 4: 434). He continues:

> Dreams are completely egoistic. Whenever my own ego does not appear in the context of the dream but only some extraneous person, I may safely assume that my own ego lies concealed by identification, behind the other person. I can insert my ego into the context. On other occasions, when my own ego does appear in the dream, the situation in which it occurs may teach me that some other person lies concealed, by identification, behind my ego. In that case the dream should warn me to transfer on to myself, when I am interpreting the dream, the concealed common element attached to this person. There are also dreams in which my ego appears along with other people who, when the identification is resolved, are revealed once again as my ego.
>
> (ibid.: 434–5)

Mikkel Borch-Jacobsen may have this passage in mind when he comments on the peculiar nature of the 'egoism' that Freud assigns to the dream-process in which the ego is both everywhere and nowhere. In *The Freudian Subject* (1989) and 'The Freudian Subject: From Politics to Ethics', first published in *October* in 1986, Borch-Jacobsen has traced Freud's theory of identification from his first systematic account of identification in *The Interpretation of Dreams* (1900) – 'Identification is not simply imitation but assimilation' (*PFL* 4: 233) – through 'Totem and Taboo' (1913), the papers on metapsychology and the Oedipus complex to the analyses of group psychology in the 1920s and 1930s. In Borch-Jacobsen's rereading, identification announces a drive towards identity, towards being an 'I', a drive which oscillates between idealization and aggression – the 'I want to be like' easily sliding into the murderous desire to replace. It is in this slide that he detects a 'primordial opacity' or non-identity that inscribes identity as such as a desire to be like and thus as fantasy. 'If I *desire* to be (an) I', he suggests in 'The Freudian Subject', 'if I *desire* myself, it must, following elementary logic, be because I am not it' (Borch-Jacobsen 1991: 66). That is, as Borch-Jacobsen had already pointed out in *The Freudian Subject*, insofar as the subject is a subject, it is only ever a subject in the fantasmatic structure of identification which is, in turn, indissociable from a dramatic structure since in fantasy 'the wish never manifests itself in the first person':

> It would be easy enough to accumulate examples, to move from dreams to hysterical fantasies, to invoke daydreams or literary fictions: everywhere we would encounter this play of ego identi-fication, always this enigmatic shifting of wish fulfilment toward another subject's pleasure.
>
> (Borch-Jacobsen 1989: 19–20)

In this sense, then, identification is bound to wish fulfilment not, or not only, through concealment – a more familiar Freudian account of a forbidden wish requiring that satisfaction is achieved under cover of being another – but through the desire for identity as such. That desire makes identification, and its subject, both collective and 'asocial' from the start. Collective because identity always takes a detour through the other or others; asocial because that detour, annihilating and devouring, threatens the being of the other. 'Identi-fication, in fact', Freud notes in 'Group Psychology and the Analysis of the Ego' (1921), 'is ambivalent from the very first; it can turn into an expression of tenderness as easily as into a wish for someone's removal' (*PFL* 12: 134). It is this insight into the ambivalence of identification, Borch-Jacobsen suggests, that Freud resists in his persistent returns to the impossible task of establishing what comes first: identification or object love. That task becomes the symptom of a psychoanalysis which tries to maintain the very subject–object distinction that it simultaneously undermines. Further, Freud's attempt to keep these two bonds distinct is symptomatic of his desire to produce a strictly triangular version of the Oedipus complex comprising an identificatory bond with the father and an object tie to the mother – an Oedipus complex, that is, which can preserve the myth of a 'primordially idyllic and harmonious sociality' (Borch-Jacobsen 1989: 182). By trying to distinguish between model and object, between identification and a post-Oedipal object love, Freud was guarding against the possibility that the aggression and indistinction between subject and other internal to identification might spill over into, and threaten to overwhelm, the social. So far as the fantasmatic structure of dreams is concerned, what is essential, for Borch-Jacobsen, 'is not the fact that the fantasmatic structure of dreams (or symptoms, or works of art) in some instances exhibits the ego although remaining silent about the identity that it usurps, while in other instances it presents an apocryphal character that the ego secretly inhabits' but that 'in every instance the ego blends its characteristics with those of an outsider, and that in this indistinction of the "I" and the "he" lies the necessary condition of every wish fulfillment' (Borch-Jacobsen 1989: 19–20).

By the same token, if the pleasures of the ego reside in the indistinction between subject and other, then we can no longer say to whom this pleasure belongs, we can no longer say whose wish is at stake – in dream, fantasy or symptom. And, recalling Mulvey, it may be too easy to describe whatever is in 'play' here as pleasure. There may, after all, be something decisive about the distinction between an identity or character that the ego takes over, or 'secretly inhabits', and an identity that carries, or 'exhibits', the ego. Freud's text does, I think, support such a distinction. There are, in fact, two different modes of identification described in the passage from *The Interpretation of Dreams*. The first refers to the apparent absence of the ego from the dream and its concealment behind, or inhabitation of, 'some extraneous person'. Freud is insistent: 'some extraneous person . . . ', 'I may safely assume . . . ', 'I can insert my ego . . .'. Or: 'Wherever I am not, I am.' These are the terms – tentatively, the terms of Borch-Jacobsen's critique of Freud – for a reading of the fantasy of identification as a non-ego identifying anyhow with anyone in the name of an identity which, however fantasmatic, however abyssal or opaque, is always there. Against this identification which makes everything the ego's own by securing every image as its reflection, the *appearance* of the ego in the dreams signals the *concealment* of another identity behind the ego, an identity with whom the ego has something in common. And, intriguingly, Freud's rhetoric changes when he describes the act, or process, of carrying another identity behind the ego. The 'some other person' is no longer just anyone and the dream is a warning about a concealed common element – a secret? – shared between the ego and the other who has come to usurp it.

The type of identification described here presents us with both a (non)identity derived, as Borch-Jacobsen has shown, from a primordial lack and a subject of, a subject *subject to*, an identification which necessarily passes through the other – that is, through the other's no less fantasmatic identifications, through the other's fantasy of itself. It is as if the desire of the other can carry the ego as its mask, can masquerade through the ego, signalling a fantasmatic and secret dispossession marked by the very visibility of the ego. Crucially disturbing the persistent association between identification, mastery and recognition, the more visible, the more recognizable, the ego becomes, the more absent it appears to be and the more it recalls Lacan's difficult and ambiguous formulation of a love for, and fascination with, the other which mutilates precisely to the extent that it aims at what is 'in you more than you' (Lacan 1979: 263). That formulation suggests why cinema's specularization of the woman, its production of the woman as 'to-be-looked-at-ness' and as visibility, is felt as a form of occupation which alienates the female spectator from her 'self'. The woman's visibility becomes a sign of the fact that she has become a mask, carrying the other's desire. In one sense, this is a masquerade of the feminine played out not, or not only, to produce a lack, or what Mary Ann Doane has described as 'a certain distance between oneself and one's image' (Doane 1982: 82), but in the name of someone else's desire – a desire taken on as the woman's 'own'.

This displacement, I would suggest, requires us to think outside of the concepts of voyeurism, fetishism and wish fulfilment which have been so central to film theory and to reread the concept of identification in relation to a cinema which seems able to solicit the type of identifications explored by Freud through the papers on metapsychology, on phylogenesis and the origins of the social tie and the sexual differentiation of the Oedipus complex. In the next chapter, I want to take a detour through Freud's work that will allow us to follow his different attempts to explain the anxious and dependent relation to the father supposedly exhibited by women and the 'masses'. For Freud, the persistent demand for love from the father defines this relation – a demand which might start to shed some light both on the different rhetorics of cinematic paternity we've been examining here and on those mass and female spectators who, always asking both for too much and not enough, seem to have so many different ways of not knowing what they want.

Chapter 3

Femininity, fantasy and the collective

(Or *Ferris Bueller's Day Off* – take two)

> She has seen it and knows that she is without it and wants to have it.
>
> (*PFL* 7: 336)

In 'Hysterical Phantasies and their Relation to Bisexuality' (1908), Freud makes a distinction between the daydreams common to men and those enjoyed by women. Daydreams, he notes, 'occur with perhaps equal frequency in both sexes' but 'it seems that while in girls and women they are invariably of an erotic nature, in men they may be either erotic or ambitious' (*PFL* 10: 87). This distinction starts to break down almost immediately as Freud goes on to draw attention to the erotic aims behind men's ambitious fantasies:

> [C]loser investigation of a man's day-dreams generally shows that all his heroic exploits are carried out and all his successes achieved only in order to please a woman and to be preferred by her to other men. These fantasies are satisfactions of wishes proceeding from deprivation and longing.
>
> (ibid.: 87)

The twist in this tale which finds a woman behind every male fantasy blurs the distinction that Freud has just introduced between masculine and feminine forms of daydream. At the same time, the observation that only men can oscillate between the ambitious and the erotic while women are 'invariably' confined to the latter, suggests a limit on, a type of fixation within, the fantasy life of the woman, a limit which reappears throughout Freud's work. The woman daydreaming to find relief from 'deprivation and longing' has something in common with the female patient of 'Analysis Terminable and Interminable' (1937) who drives Freud to distraction because she persists in her 'unrealizable' demand for a penis, or with the woman of 30 described in 'Femininity' in 1933, who, unlike the 'youthful, somewhat unformed' man of the same age, 'frightens us by her psychical rigidity and unchangeability. Her libido has taken up final positions and seems incapable of exchanging them for others' (Freud 1963: 270; 1933: 133–4).

This sketch of the relation between a female patient 'insusceptible to influence' because she is, Freud tells us, 'exhausted' by the difficulty of femininity itself and the analyst confronted by a woman who terrifies him because she knows only one mind presents another side of that history of psychoanalysis, sometimes told as a more or less loving, more or less seductive encounter between Freud and his women. Acknowledging that his comments do not always 'sound friendly', Freud asks his readers not to forget that he has only been describing women's nature as it is 'determined by their sexual function', as if whatever it is that is specific to feminine sexuality is responsible for the failure to relinquish the positions taken up by women's libido. In a now infamous passage, Freud links that failure to women's 'weaker' social interests:

> The fact that women must be regarded as having little sense of justice is no doubt related to the predominance of envy in their mental life; for the demand for justice is a modification of envy and lays down the condition subject to which one can put envy aside. We also regard women as weaker in their social interests and as having less capacity for sublimating their instincts than men. The former is no doubt derived from the dissocial quality which unquestionably characterizes all sexual relations.
>
> (Freud 1933: 134)

In her extensive critique of Freud's paper on 'Femininity', Luce Irigaray insists that the 'fact that women are "weaker in their social interests" is obvious. The ambiguity, the double meaning, of that expression makes further comment unnecessary' (Irigaray 1985: 119) – a refusal to comment which leaves us in no doubt that women's supposed lack of interest in the social is being reinflected as a source of potential resistance to 'a society in which they have no stake' (ibid.). But what Freud has to say about the dissocial quality of femininity – a dissociality he immediately associates with the 'psychical rigidity' of the 30-year-old woman – can be used to examine the difference that psychoanalysis claims to detect in feminine fantasy. This passage is part of a discussion of the 'weak' feminine superego in which Freud sets out the sexual differentiation of the castration complex:

> In the absence of fear of castration the chief motive is lacking which leads boys to surmount the Oedipus complex. Girls remain in it for an indeterminate length of time; they demolish it late and, even so, incompletely. In these circumstances the formation of the super-ego must suffer; it cannot attain the strength and independence which give it its cultural significance, and feminists are not pleased when we point out to them the effects of this factor upon the average feminine character.
>
> (Freud 1933: 129)

Here Freud's reference to the feminists anticipates the difficulty that this description of the feminine superego has presented to a feminism which turns to psychoanalysis for a description of the woman's relation to the social bond. For now I want to note that the feminine superego suffers – and, recalling Irigaray, to keep the ambiguity of that expression. The legacy of the girl's passage through the Oedipus complex is an exorbitant demand for a penis, a demand that will never, it seems, go away. In a cluster of papers published between 1923 and 1933 – 'The Infantile Genital Organization' (1923), 'The Dissolution of the Oedipus Complex' (1924), 'Some Psychical Consequences of the Anatomical Distinction Between the Sexes' (1925), 'Female Sexuality' (1931) and 'Femininity' (1933) – Freud analysed the feminine form of the Oedipus complex to account both for the girl's sexual difference, her femininity, and for her deformed relation to the social function. 'I cannot evade the notion', he notes in 1925,

> (though I hesitate to give it expression) that for women the level of what is ethically normal is different from what it is in men. Their super-ego is never so inexorable, so impersonal, so independent of its emotional origins as we require it to be in men.
>
> (*PFL* 7: 342)

In the classical Freudian schema, the girl's sexual and social difference is taken back to the fact that she lacks not only a penis but the narcissistic investment in the penis which mobilizes a masculine and social submission to the paternal prohibition against incest:

In boys . . . the complex is not simply repressed, it is literally
smashed to pieces by the shock of threatened castration . . . In
normal, or, it is better to say, in ideal cases, the Oedipus complex
exists no longer, even in the unconscious: the super-ego has
become its heir . . . [T]he catastrophe to the Oedipus complex (the
abandonment of incest and the institution of conscience and
morality) may be regarded as a victory of the race over the
individual.

(*PFL* 7: 341)

All this because the little boy loves his penis more than his mother
or his father, more than the family which Freud was so used to
describing as a site of feminized resistance to the civilizing influence
of social ties (see, for example, 'Civilisation and its Discontents',
PFL 12: 293). There is no distinction here between loving the penis
and loving the collective, an indistinction that puts masculine
narcissism to social effect by handing the boy over to the 'race'. The
lack, or worse, the loss, represented by the girl's genitals confirms
the boy's belief in the 'reality' of castration and thus secures his
identification with the Oedipal law – the law which states the father's
prohibition against incest with the mother and the father for the boy
who has then to establish himself as both social (not incestuous) and
heterosexual (not perverse). Because he fears the loss of his penis,
the boy renounces both his rivalry with his father and his homosexual
desire for him. The shock of the sight of the girl's lack will never
really go away, it may 'permanently determine the boy's relation to
women: horror of the mutilated creature or triumphant contempt for
her' (*PFL* 7: 336) and it will guide him through the dissolution of
the Oedipus complex.

It's worth noting that elsewhere Freud was careful to insist that
nothing in the psyche ever goes away, that 'where the libido is
concerned, man . . . [shows] himself incapable of giving up a
satisfaction he has once enjoyed' (*PFL* 11: 88). The possibility that
a desire can be wiped out is enough to skew not only the reconstruction of the analysand's history but a psychoanalytic theory of
individual and group identity based on the repression and sublimation of drives which can only guarantee the subject and the social
insofar as they don't go away. This is, perhaps, the stake of the
'ideal' or exceptional nature of the masculine superego which Freud
is so anxious to differentiate from the feminine formation. How else
are we to account for the absolute loss, the radical destruction, at the

centre of Freud's concept of an ideal superego structured by both the perceived absence of the female genitals and the abolition, from within, of the desire for the Oedipal love objects. That abolition seems to repeat, in idealized form, the trauma of what Freud insisted on calling the woman's lack of a penis – the shock of a look which generates the boy's fear of dispossession is transformed, through the superego, into his accession to, and inheritance of, the social itself. In the unstable form of an 'internal instead of an external dependence', a 'self-reliance' which is at the same time a 'true, pre-eminently conservative' tie to civilization, Freud recognizes the masculine superego: 'People of this type are dominated by fear of their conscience instead of fear of losing love' ('Libidinal Types', 1931; *PFL* 7: 362).

The fragility of Freud's analysis at this point makes itself felt in his more or less antagonistic disrespect for the 'mutilated' feminine superego. It is as if the stress of masculine identification with the paternal law reappears as the degradation of the feminine superego characterized by a demand for love which leaves it, very precisely, in a state of 'uncivilized' external dependence. In girls 'the Oedipus complex escapes the fate which it meets with in boys: it may be slowly abandoned or dealt with by repression, or its effects may persist far into women's normal mental life' (*PFL* 7: 342). If the woman ever does give up her incestuous love objects, Freud suggested in 'The Dissolution of the Oedipus Complex' in 1924, it will be the result of 'upbringing and of intimidation from outside which threatens her with a loss of love' (*PFL* 7: 321). More typically, she continues to make a demand for love on the father who thereby remains a pressing reality in the life of the daughter: 'Every analyst has come across certain women who cling with especial intensity and tenacity to the attachment to their father and to the wish in which it culminates in having a child by him' (*PFL* 7: 335). There is, then, no Oedipal 'catastrophe' to come between the daughter and her exorbitant demand for love – sometimes, again infamously, commuted to baby or penis – from the father. Her demand can persist unless and until the girl is intimidated into renouncing it, a renunciation which then faces her with a pernicious double bind – either to give up her paternal love object because she fears losing his love or to exchange loving her father for being loved by him.[1] Either way, the girl is made over to a pressure from outside, to the pressure of paternal threat and/or paternal love.

It is from this point that the concept of the feminine superego can be used to clarify the distinctive preoccupations of and with both femininity and feminine fantasy which show up through Freud's work from the *Studies on Hysteria* with Josef Breuer in the 1890s to the analyses of the structure of sexual difference, social identification and of mass psychology in the 1920s and 1930s. In *Studies on Hysteria*, Freud and Breuer's 'friendliness', their sympathetic attention to the intelligence and morality of their female analysands, is in contrast to what can so easily appear as Freud's repudiation of both women and femininity in his analysis of the dependent feminine supercgo and women's demanding identification, or lack of it, with the social. In one sense, and very schematically, the description of the feminine superego can be understood as the effect of a theoretical reversal in which the father's asocial tie to the daughter is reinflected as her degraded identification with the socializing function of the paternal. In the 1890s, as Freud starts to derive the hysterical symptom from a real sexual encounter experienced as shock, the paradigmatic and scandalous emotional tie uncovered by psychoanalysis is the one between a perverse father and his hysterical daughter. In *Studies on Hysteria*, that tie breaks through the veil of discretion which Freud and Breuer drew over their published case histories in the form of cryptic and undecidable stories about fathers, somewhere between insane and overfond, who 'love' their daughters with a special intimacy:

> she gave way to the extent of letting fall a single significant phrase; but she had hardly said a word before she stopped, and her old father, who was sitting behind her, began to sob bitterly.

> I venture after the lapse of so many years to lift the veil of discretion and reveal the fact that Katharina was not the niece but the daughter of the landlady. The girl fell ill, therefore, as a result of sexual attempts on the part of her own father.

> In this instance, too, it was in fact the girl's father, not her uncle.
> (*PFL* 3: 162; 201; 242)

Thus, in the *Studies* and, more overtly, in 'The Aetiology of Hysteria' (1896), Freud theorized a father who threatened psychoanalysis with a public scandal, whose libidinal attentions produced neither Oedipal law nor social identification but an omission or a wish to forget. '[T]he nature of the trauma', Freud wrote in 1893, 'excluded a reaction . . . it was a question of things which the patient wished to forget, and therefore intentionally repressed from his conscious thought' – a repression which dissociates memory from affect to produce the hysterical symptom (*PFL* 3: 61). A famous passage from 'The Aetiology of Hysteria' sets out Freud's point of departure from more accepted, and acceptable, accounts of sexuality and sexual experience in childhood:

> It seems to me certain that our children are far more often exposed to sexual assaults than the few precautions taken by parents in this connection would lead us to expect. When I first made enquiries about what was known on the subject, I learnt from colleagues that there are several publications by paediatricians which stigmatize the frequency of sexual practices by nurses and nursery maids, carried out even on infants in arms . . . [T]he findings of my analysis are in a position to speak for themselves. In all eighteen cases (cases of pure hysteria and of hysteria combined with obsessions, and comprising six men and twelve women) I have, as I have said, come to learn of sexual experiences of this kind in childhood.
>
> (Freud 1896, cited in Masson 1984: 267–8)

Read back onto the *Studies on Hysteria*, 'Aetiology' marks every case there as the effect of a sexual assault or seduction – 'all eighteen cases' so far analysed confirm Freud's estimation of the frequency of sexual abuse in childhood. Freud's conclusion is stark – '[A]t the bottom of every case of hysteria there are one or more occurrences of premature sexual experience' (ibid.: 263) – and, as he wrote to Wilhelm Fliess a month after reading the paper to variously bewildered, outraged and silent members of the Society for Psychiatry and Neurology in Vienna in April 1896, it left him 'as isolated as you could wish me to be' (Masson 1984: 10).

There is a gap of more than twenty years between the perversity of a father who subjects his daughter to an illegitimate demand for sexual intimacy and the dissociality of a femininity which refuses to relinquish its demand for love on a father who now lays down the Oedipal law. More specifically, the perverse or degraded father of the seduction theory gives way before the aggrandized figure of Narcissus – the primal father of 'Totem and Taboo' (1913) and 'Group Psychology and the Analysis of the Ego' (1921) through whom Freud constructs his myth of the patricidal origin of the social. Thus there is a shift through Freud's text from the perverse to the narcissistic father which coincides with a gradual relinquishment of what has been described as the 'respectful attitude of sympathetic understanding' towards the women to whom Freud owed the initial discoveries of psychoanalysis (Appignanesi and Forrester 1992: 5). To put this another way: Freud's attempts to analyse and to describe the concept of femininity are thoroughly implicated in, if not indissociable from, the vicissitudes of the paternal through his psychoanalytic theory.

That implication is only at its most obvious in Jeffrey Masson's attack on psychoanalysis in *Freud: The Assault on Truth*, published in 1984. Masson writes the history of psychoanalysis as a story of betrayal and suppression – Freud's betrayal of abused women and children from the moment he 'renounces' the seduction theory in the name of infantile fantasy. His argument equates the seduction theory with an ethical recognition of an 'important truth: the sexual, physical and emotional violence that is a real and tragic part of the lives of many children' (Masson 1984: 189). In Masson's account, Freud's elaboration of the psychoanalytic theory of fantasy as such is undertaken only at the cost of undermining the truth value of the woman's utterance. Similarly, Freud's increasing lack of confidence in the seduction theory is understood simply as his refusal either to publicly stand by his discovery of a traumatic sexual reality or to make the type of accusation against the father that such a discovery seems to demand. The letter to Fliess in which Freud confesses that 'I no longer believe in my neurotica' is quoted in full by Masson for whom it 'symbolizes the beginning of an internal reconciliation with his colleagues and with the whole of nineteenth century psychiatry' (ibid.: 108; 110). Put crudely, for Masson it is at this moment that psychoanalysis succumbs to the pressure of patriarchy and gives up its essential insight into sexual violence within the family. Because that insight is grounded in both the truth value of the patient's utterance and an adequation between 'what happens' and the representation of the real event in memory and language, both are lost to psychoanalysis from the moment that Freud writes to Fliess concerning his 'certain insight that there are no indications of reality in the unconscious, so that one cannot distinguish between truth and fiction that has been cathected with affect' (cited by Masson 1984: 109). Masson is clear that this indistinction between truth and affective fiction has undermined, and continues to undermine, psychoanalytic theory and practice. Freud may have believed he was

> doing the right thing ... when he shifted his attention from external trauma to internal fantasy as the causative agent in mental

illness. But this does not mean it represents the truth . . . [I]t is unforgivable that those entrusted with the lives of people who come to them in emotional pain, having suffered real wounds in childhood, should use their blind reliance on Freud's fearful abandonment of the seduction theory to continue the abuse their patients once suffered as children.

(ibid.: 189;192)

The suggestion is that Freud's cowardly turn to fantasy locks the daughter (most typically) into the incestuous and masochistic corruption of her fantasy life and exonerates the fathers by eliminating the traumatized reality of the emotional and sexual tie they have demanded. At this point, psychoanalysis itself becomes more or less indistinguishable from rape – an indistinction which could then be used, if we followed the logic of Masson's argument, to make a familiar sense out of the apparent shift from the perverse to the social father in Freud's theory as neither more nor less than the effect of the progressive conservatism of psychoanalysis, its submission to the fantasy of a loving and totalitarian Narcissus which obscures the perversity of the social process. But there is an obvious sense in which whatever is taking place in Freud's text between the seduction theory and the elaborations of Oedipal and social identification is more complicated than this. It can, and has been, argued that Freud never simply gave up his interest in 'external trauma' in the name of infantile fantasy (Laplanche and Pontalis 1986; Davidson 1984; Rose 1986). The footnotes to *Studies on Hysteria* identifying the father as the perpetrator of a sexual assault were added to the published text in 1924, nearly thirty years after Freud is supposed to have renounced the seduction theory. It is also evident from the following passage from 'The Aetiology of Hysteria' that the opposition between fantasy and the real event/seduction theory imposed by Masson's reading cannot account for the difficult implication of memory, fantasy and reality encountered by Freud in the early stages of psychoanalysis:

We have learned that *no hysterical symptom can arise from a real experience alone, but that in every case the memory of earlier experiences awakened in association to it plays a part in causing the symptom* . . . You will moreover notice the consistency with which the proposition that symptoms can only proceed from memories is carried through in hysteria. None of the later scenes, in which the symptoms arise, are the effective ones; and the experiences which are effective have at first no result.

(Freud, cited in Masson 1984: 257; 273–4)

Even here, then, in the paper cited by Masson as proof that Freud had once believed in the reality of sexual trauma, it is never simply a question of isolating the original trauma outside of memory and representation. But Masson systematically obscures the role assigned to memory in the construction of the symptom and emphasized by Freud in both 'Aetiology' and the 'Project for a Scientific Psychology' – described by Laplanche and Pontalis as 'the best point of access to what is most original in the Freudian theory of memory' (Laplanche and Pontalis 1973: 248). Freud was working on the 'Project' through 1895. 'I am positively devoured by it, till I am really overworked and have to break off. I have never experienced such a powerful preoccupation', he confided in a letter to Fliess in April that year and, a month later, on 25 May:

I have devoted every minute of the last few weeks to work like this; I have spent the night hours from eleven till two with imaginings, transpositions and guesses like these . . . You will have to wait a long time yet for any results.

(*SE* 1: 283; 284)

Just over two weeks later, on 12 June, he wrote again to Fliess:

[the] psychological construction looks as though it would succeed, which would give me immense pleasure. Of course nothing certain can be said as yet. To make an announcement on this now would be like sending the six-months' foetus of a girl to a ball.

(ibid.)

The strange and carefully sexually differentiated body which lends this simile both its pathos and its violence is, in one sense, a prototype of the body and psyche described in the 'Project' – a body and psyche overwhelmed by a more or less violent stimulation, both from without and within, that it must either lose or resist and register. The 'Project' was finally sent to Fliess in October 1895. A long letter revising its contents followed in January 1896. Then, as the editor to the *Standard Edition* notes in a Preface, 'the "Project" disappears from view till its re-emergence some fifty years later with the rest of Freud's forgotten letters to Fliess. Only the ideas contained in it persisted, and eventually blossomed out into the theories of psychoanalysis' (ibid.: 286). First published posthumously in 1950 and included in the first volume of the *Standard Edition* as an example of Freud's 'Scientific and Pre-Psychoanalytic Writings' (although it post-dates the *Studies on Hysteria* usually considered one of the founding texts of psychoanalysis), the 'Project' finds its mutilated place between neurology and psychoanalysis. Whatever its claims to anticipate the 'blossoming' of psychoanalysis proper, however effectively its 'invisible ghost' has 'haunt[ed] the whole series of Freud's theoretical writings to the very end', the 'Project' remains – 'must remain', Strachey insists – 'a torso disavowed by its creator' (ibid.: 290; 293). Freud 'seems to have forgotten it or at least never to have referred to it. And when in his old age he was presented with it afresh, he did his best to destroy it' (ibid.: 290).

I don't think we can understand Freud's certainty that there are 'no indications of reality in the unconscious', that it is impossible to distinguish in the psyche 'between truth and fiction that has been cathected with affect' outside of the psychical economy of resistance, breaching and registration of mnemic traces set out in the 'Project'. In the 'Project', as Laplanche and Pontalis have pointed out,

> Freud attempts to account for the registration of the memory in the neuronal apparatus without making any appeal to a resemblance between trace and object. The memory-trace is simply a particular arrangement of facilitations, so organized that one route is followed in preference to another.
>
> (Laplanche and Pontalis 1973: 248)

In the opening section of the 'Project', Freud describes memory as a main characteristic of nervous tissue and defines memory as 'quite generally, a capacity for being permanently altered by single occurrences – which offers such a striking contrast to the behaviour of a material that permits the passage of a wave-movement and thereafter returns to its former condition'. He continues:

> A psychological theory deserving any consideration must furnish an explanation of 'memory'. Now any such explanation comes up against the difficulty that it must assume on the one hand that neurones are permanently different after an excitation from what they were before, while nevertheless it cannot be disputed that, in general, fresh excitations meet with the same conditions of

reception as did the earlier ones. It would seem, therefore, that neurones must be both influenced and also unaltered, unprejudiced. Thus there are *permeable* neurones (offering no resistance and retaining nothing), which serve for perception, and *impermeable* ones (loaded with resistance, and holding back Qn), which are the vehicles of memory and so probably of psychical processes in general.

(*SE* 1: 299–300)

I've quoted this passage extensively because it sets out so clearly the preoccupations, the 'imaginings, transpositions and guesses', which provoke Freud into that unusually sickening image of a six-months' foetus of a girl at a ball in order to describe the theoretical prematurity of his 'psychological construction'. At the same time, this is, as Laplanche stresses in *Life and Death in Psychoanalysis*, a 'clinical model. What animates the model and makes it something different from a purely speculative construct is the clinical experience of a still emerging psychoanalysis and the rather strange phenomena it observes' (Laplanche 1976: 55). For example, the case of 'Emma' in the 'Project' is used by Freud to demonstrate the explanatory force of his theory of memory. Emma suffers from a compulsion of not being able to go into shops alone. She produces two scenes, or memories, in relation to this. The first, when she was 12, describes two shop assistants laughing at her. She 'ran away in some kind of affect of fright. In connection with this, she was led to recall that the two of them were laughing at her clothes and that one of them had pleased her sexually' (*SE* 1: 353). Describing the scene as strictly unintelligible, Freud pressed on with his investigation. Emma recounts a second memory: 'On two occasions when she was a child of eight she had gone into a small shop to buy some sweets, and the shopkeeper had grabbed at her genitals through her clothes.' In spite of this, she had gone back to the shop: 'She now reproached herself for having gone there the second time, as though she had wanted in that way to provoke the assault' (ibid.: 354). Only the association between these two scenes, Freud insists, can explain the affect of fright in the first memory: 'In the shop the two assistants were laughing; this laughing aroused (unconsciously) the memory of the shopkeeper'; further, and crucially: 'The memory [i.e. of the first shopkeeper] aroused what it was certainly not able to at the time, a sexual release, which was transformed into anxiety' (ibid.). He summarizes his conclusion as follows:

Here we have the case of a memory arousing an affect which it did not arouse as an experience, because in the meantime the change [brought about] in puberty had made possible a different understanding of what was remembered. Now this case is typical of repression in hysteria. We invariably find that a memory is repressed which has only become a trauma by deferred action.

(*SE* 1: 356)

Masson glosses this conclusion as evidence that Freud was concerned with real, traumatic events in the 'Project', with memories of scenes that 'beyond any question . . . actually took place' (Masson 1984: 89). This being 'beyond question' then legitimates what Jacqueline Rose has called an 'unequivocal accusation of the real' in Masson's reading (Rose 1986: 12). It is an accusation which does not – perhaps cannot – acknowledge the chronic undecidability introduced into the relation between event, memory and representation by the concept of deferred action, that is, by a model of the relation between the psyche and the 'outside' which allows for a dissociation between affect and 'experience', or trace and object. That dissociation puts affect into a type of circulation which allows both and equally for the possibility of traumas without affect and for memories of events that have never been. Again, this is no simple, or single, opposition between fantasy and reality, between telling the truth and telling lies, and it cannot be used, as it is by Masson, to make the 'Project' innocent in its relation to the bodies and speech of women and children and 'truthful' in its accusation of the paternal compared to Freud's later work. At the same time, to say that innocence has been established too quickly is not to suggest that another accusation needs to be made against an as yet concealed and silent abuse within the 'Project'. On the contrary, what Freud does in the 'Project' seems to me to go beyond a logic of accusation and defence; or rather, the structure of memory he starts to propose there confounds that logic in all its certainty of who does what to whom and why.

It should also be said that the implication of affect, memory and event which Freud was uncovering through the language of hysteria did not prevent him from making a decision about the reality of sexual abuse – work on the 'Project' precedes the 'Aetiology'. Something else intervenes in that decision and it is not, or not only, the real event which is under threat but the theory of memory that supports, or facilitates, the specificity of a psychoanalytic theory of fantasy and of representation. Jean Laplanche and Jean-Bertrand Pontalis have also questioned a standard account of the development of psychoanalysis which links the displacement of the seduction theory to the discovery of the Oedipus complex and unconscious fantasy. In his published works at least, Freud turned neither to the Oedipal drama nor to the processes of fantasy but to the sexual development of the child and the determining role of the sexual constitution. The following passage from 'My Views on the Part Played by Sexuality in the Aetiology of the Neuroses' (1906), in which Freud formally qualifies his allegiance to the seduction theory, indicates something of what is at stake in the shift from the seduction theory to an endogenous infantile sexuality:

> I was at that period unable to distinguish with certainty between falsifications made by hysterics in their memories of childhood and traces of real events. Since then I have learned to explain a number of phantasies of seduction as attempts at fending off memories of the subject's own sexual activity (infantile mastur-bation). When this point had been clarified, the 'traumatic' element in the sexual experiences of childhood lost its importance and what was left was the realization that infantile sexual activity (whether spontaneous or provoked) prescribes the direction that will be taken by later sexual life after maturity.
>
> (*PFL* 10: 75)

With the occlusion of the accidents of individual history by a spontaneous infantile sexuality, a type of biological realism moves centre-stage in Freud's theory – a realism to which memory, fantasy and even the event can then only ever be secondary. Whether 'spontaneous or provoked', whether the child is left to discover its 'own' sexuality or precipitated into what Freud had described as a pre-sexual sexual experience, seems to make no difference here: sexuality will find its own way and drag the psyche along with it. In 'Fantasy and the Origins of Sexuality', Laplanche and Pontalis have also suggested that infantile sexuality is conceived as biological reality because Freud is at first unable to articulate that sexuality with the Oedipus complex. The Oedipus complex is not formally introduced into Freud's theory until 1910, in 'A Special Type of Object-Choice Made by Men', though it is clearly in use before then (Laplanche and Pontalis 1973: 283). As we've seen, not until the 1920s does Freud start to discuss the 'full' Oedipus complex (in which both sexes take up active and passive incestuous positions in relation to both parents) in all its sexually and socially differentiated complexity.

Thus the theoretical reversal which transforms the father's illegitimate demand on the daughter into her fixated and unrealizable demand for love from him takes place – if it can be said to take place – over a period of twenty years which see not only Freud's initial turn to a biological realism but the development of the phylogenetic theory worked out through 'Totem and Taboo' (1912), 'Group Psychology and the Analysis of the Ego' (1921), the recently discovered 'Overview of the Transference Neuroses' (c. 1915) and the key papers on metapsychology – 'On Narcissism' (1914), 'Mourning and Melancholia' (1917) and 'The Ego and the Id' (1923). This passing, I want to suggest, shows up in Freud's theory of femininity – more precisely, in the melancholic mode of identification that he assigns to femininity whenever the woman's relation to the father is in question. Freud makes explicit the connection between the feminine superego and melancholia in 'The Ego and the Id' in 1923 when he notes that a properly superegoic identification with the lost Oedipal objects does not result in the *incorporation* of those objects into the ego – the incorporation which he has previously described as typical of melancholia – at least in the boy: '[T]his alternative outcome may also occur, and is easier to observe in girls than in boys' (*PFL* 11: 372). Freud had already argued, in 'Mourning and Melancholia' in 1917, that the melancholic regresses from object-cathexis to identification by incorporating inside the ego an object which has been lost or abandoned 'owing to a real slight or disappointment coming from this loved person' (*PFL* 11: 257). That disappointment shatters the ego's relation to an object which had been cathected on a narcissistic basis and object-libido is withdrawn back onto the ego. Once withdrawn, however,

> it was not employed in any unspecified way, but served to establish an identification of the ego with the abandoned object. Thus the shadow of the object fell upon the ego, and the latter could henceforth be judged by a special agency as though it were an object, the forsaken object.
>
> (ibid.: 258)

In melancholia, the pleasures of a spectacular self-abasement derive from the aggression generated by a conflict between the ego and its love object which has split the ego in two – into an ego 'altered by identification' and the critical agency to which it

succumbs. But this formulation occludes the uncertainty or indecision worrying at Freud's attempts to analyse the mechanism of
melancholic loss, an uncertainty which takes the form of an inability
to state precisely what it is the melancholic has lost in his or her
object. On the one hand, melancholic identification transforms an
object loss into an ego loss in the name of a love that cannot be given
up even in – especially in – the face of the degradation of its object.
On the other hand, the melancholic who loses her or his own ego
does not know what she, or he, has lost in the other, does not know
what it is that has generated the desire to incorporate the other, put
it in the place of the ego and then abuse it. The object 'has not
perhaps actually died', Freud speculates, but has been lost as a love
object, 'e.g. in the case of a betrothed girl who has been jilted'. In
other cases, there seems to have been a similar type of loss 'but one
cannot see clearly what it is that has been lost, and it is all the more
reasonable to suppose that the patient cannot consciously perceive
what he has lost either':

> This, indeed, might be so even if the patient is aware of the loss
> which has given rise to this melancholia, but only in the sense that
> he knows *whom* he has lost but not *what* he has lost in him. This
> would suggest that melancholia is in some way related to an object-
> loss which is withdrawn from consciousness, in contradistinction
> to mourning, in which there is nothing about the loss that is
> unconscious.
>
> (ibid.: 253–4)

The desire to know what has been lost and why always risks
turning the theorization of melancholia into a scene of accusation
and retribution which precisely reproduces the psychical relation
between the ego and its critical agency through the question: whose
fault is it? What extravagant demand has the melancholic made that
was bound either to issue in disappointment, real or imaginary, or to
drive the loved object away? Or: what shame has degraded the object
so much that the only way of sustaining its narcissistic value is to
incorporate it and exchange it for the ego itself? The melancholic
seems to present Freud with a moment of excessive loss – loss that,
in 1923, he then carefully transfers onto the feminine superego. The
dissolution of the Oedipus complex for the boy, the absolute
destruction of the incestuous object-relation which forms his masculine and social superego, may appear to involve the type of object
loss that would usually solicit an alteration of the ego 'which can

only be described as a setting up of the object inside the ego, as it occurs in melancholia' (*PFL* 11: 368). But, Freud insists, it takes place without incorporation of the incestuous objects:

> These identifications are not what we should have expected [from the previous account], since they do not introduce the abandoned object into the ego; but this alternative outcome may also occur, and is easier to observe in girls than in boys. Analysis very often shows that a little girl, after she has had to relinquish her father as a love-object, will bring her masculinity into prominence and identify herself with her father (that is, with the object which has been lost), instead of with her mother. This will clearly depend on whether the masculinity in her disposition – whatever that may consist in – is strong enough.
>
> (ibid.: 372)

In other words, the more the girl identifies with her father, with her (or his) masculinity, the more feminine and the less social she becomes – as if by overwhelming herself with the paternal she can only remain disaffected from its Oedipal prohibition. Reading across from 'Mourning and Melancholia' to 'The Ego and the Id', we can see that the feminine superego leaves the woman open to a melancholic relation to the other and to the suffering of an ego driven to death by a superego embodying the 'pure culture of the death instinct' (ibid.: 394). In 'The Blind Spot of an Old Dream of Symmetry' (referred to briefly at the beginning of this chapter), Luce Irigaray sets out what is perhaps the most elaborate series of crosschecks between the symptoms of melancholia and the libidinal economy of the girl: *profoundly painful dejection*; *abrogation of interest in the outside world*; *loss of the capacity for love*; *inhibition of all activity*; *fall in self-esteem* (Irigaray 1985: 66–7). Above all, the 'open wound' (*PFL* 11: 262) of a melancholically impoverished ego and the 'wound to her narcissism' (*PFL* 7: 337) suffered by the girl when she discovers that she lacks the penis draw melancholia and femininity together until they are almost indistinguishable. But Irigaray pulls back from a fully melancholic occupation of femininity when she suggests that the woman 'will not choose melancholia as her privileged form of withdrawal' because 'she probably does not have the capacity for narcissism great enough to allow her to fall back on melancholia' (Irigaray 1985: 71). Instead she returns the woman to hysteria as the only possible 'remainder' for feminine lack – a lack so absolute that the woman does not even have enough narcissism to participate in either of Freud's two exemplary modes of melancholic preoccupation with the object: 'In the two opposed situations of being most intensely in love and of suicide the ego is overwhelmed by the object, though in totally different ways' (*PFL* 11: 261).

If we follow Freud's thinking through the papers on the sexual differentiation of the Oedipus complex, then the woman would have to lack the form of narcissism that Irigaray appears to have in mind when she draws attention to Freud's comment that the melancholic, while denouncing himself as worthless, is 'far from evincing towards those around [him] . . . the attitude of humility and submission' that we might expect (Freud, cited in Irigaray 1985: 69). While Irigaray makes an oblique reference to the 'economy of female narcissism and the fragility of the girl's or the woman's ego', she does not spell out precisely how this economy makes it 'impossible for the melancholic syndrome to establish a firm and dominant foundation' (ibid.: 71). Tentatively, the emphasis in Irigaray's critique on the woman's lack of narcissism tends to occlude the very specific form of feminine narcissism outlined by Freud in 'On Narcissism' in 1914. It is not that there is no such thing as a narcissistic femininity for Freud. On the contrary, the weak feminine superego mirrors, or depends on, a narcissism which he finds, almost comically, typical of women, cats and children. For the Freud of 'On Narcissism', in fact, the 'purest and truest' type of woman is the woman who, especially if she grows up with 'good looks', enjoys a certain 'self-contentment':

> Strictly speaking, it is only themselves that such women love with an intensity comparable to that of the man's love for them. Nor does their need lie in the direction of loving but of being loved; and the man who fulfils this condition is the one who finds favour with them. The importance of this type of woman for the erotic life of mankind is to be rated very high.
>
> (*PFL* 11: 82)

Freud seems here to submit to, rather than to analyse, the supposed 'great charm of narcissistic women' who cause their lovers such unease with their 'enigmatic natures' and doubtful capacity for loving back (ibid.: 83). That submission then gives us an account of an eroticized feminine narcissism defined not so much as love of the self – or of a privileged part of the self – but as the 'need' to be loved without loving back. Even the most narcissistic femininity, that is, remains dependent on an external other; it cannot mobilize, or take refuge in, the independence and self-sufficiency which Freud ascribes both to narcissism and to the superego in their masculine forms. The woman has the wrong kind of narcissism – a 'mistaken' narcissism invested not in her genitals but in the looks which may fascinate the father and the rest of 'mankind' but are not enough to save her from having to ask someone, whether father, brother or lover, to make up for her singular lack from the outside. Taking the form of a demand for love, feminine narcissism becomes a shared or common element between the woman and an other to whom she is, in effect, made over, an other who is always, in the final instance of the classical Freudian schema, the father.[2]

Following a profoundly melancholic logic, then, the woman's demand for love submits her to the outside, to the other and to the father so that, rather than the woman's lack of narcissism protecting her against melancholia, it is precisely her feminine narcissism which opens her up to melancholia and to the 'suffering' of the feminine superego. In his account of the melancholic under the spell of an agonizing attraction in which the ego is lost to, or overwhelmed by, an object that it cannot bear to lose, Freud traces the mechanism of an occupation suspended somewhere between fascination and suicide. At the same time, the melancholic structure of the feminine superego defines the sexual difference of femininity at the moment of its traumatized (over)identification with, and exclusion from, the socializing function of the father. What starts to become quite painfully clear at this point is that, for Freud, 'femininity' is taken on as both a sexed and a social identity, as sexual difference and as a deformed relation to the social. That deformation is then given a crucial elaboration, for us, in the papers on group, or mass, psychology and identification. The potential for suffering written into the feminine superego is shared, for example, with the mass superego described in 'Civilization and its Discontents' in 1930. Freud derives the mass superego from the primordial and constitutive aggression internal to the infantile ego, an aggression which that ego directs against a parental authority which demands renunciation of its instinctual satisfactions. The infant's biological vulnerability turns that aggression into anxiety which finds expression in the fear of being abandoned and left to die. That fear then becomes the prototype of the social anxiety that Freud always distinguishes from a properly masculine and guilty identification with the social. First, he insists,

comes renunciation of instinct owing to fear of aggression by the
external authority. (This is, of course, what fear of the loss of love
amounts to, for love is a protection against this punitive aggression.) After that comes the erection of an internal authority, and
renunciation of instinct owing to fear of it – owing to fear of
conscience.

(*PFL* 12: 320)

Apparently attached to a type of *Massenpsychologie* at this point,
Freud is clear that both women and the masses fail to reach this
second stage:

[I]n many adults . . . it [social anxiety] has only changed to the
extent that the place of the father or the two parents is taken by
the larger human community . . . Present-day society has to reckon
in general with this state of mind.

(ibid.: 317)

Just as the girl will be induced to give up her incestuous desires only
by a threat of the loss of love that comes from the outside – most
drastically, from the father whose love she solicits – so the masses
are social only in the sense that they respond to a fear of retribution.
Thus the feminine superego, the type of collective identification
marked as feminine, lines up on the side of the mass in its
dependence on a 'real' object and its social anxiety – an anxiety
which suggests, in turn, that the woman's narcissistic demand for
love is something like a demand for proof that she is not going to be
left to die. In this sense, too, the narcissistic woman, or the father's
daughter, becomes the prototype of the anxious mass subject of
'Civilization and its Discontents' as the mass and the feminine are
mapped onto one another to represent a degraded form of collective
identification and, though it amounts to the same thing, a traumatized
relation to the father.

When Freud discusses the relation between women and fathers,
then, it is either to oscillate between a theory of the hysterical
symptom as the effect of a perverse father or as the staging of a
fantasy about a seductive one or to express doubts about women's
ability to identify with the paternal as a social function at all. In both
a weak and a strong sense, this is a melancholic scenario: it is sad
and it is inseparable from a type of occupation, or preoccupation,
written into femininity by psychoanalysis. The mechanism and the
effect of this preoccupation on Freud's theories of femininity and

fantasy in collective identification can be clarified further through the phylogenetic fantasies set out in 'Totem and Taboo' and 'Overview of the Transference Neuroses' (c. 1915). In 'Totem and Taboo', Freud describes the primal father as the head of a horde of women and young or castrated males. Adult males are driven out of the horde in the name of the father's right to all the women of the group. In an act of rebellion against this monopoly, the males return to kill and eat the father, a murder and an incorporation which secure the origin of the social tie through an identification with the wishes of the now dead father:

> After they had got rid of him, had satisfied their hatred and had put into effect their wish to identify themselves with him, the affection which had all this time been pushed under was bound to make itself felt. It did so in the form of remorse . . . The dead father became stronger than the living one had been – for events took the course we so often see them follow in human affairs to this day. What had up to then been prevented by his actual existence was thenceforward prohibited by the sons themselves, in accordance with the psychological procedure so familiar to us in psycho-analyses under the name of 'deferred obedience'. They revoked their deed by forbidding the killing of the totem, the substitute for their father; and they renounced its fruits by resigning their claim to the women who had now been set free.
>
> (*PFL* 13: 204–5)

The death of the primal father institutes the two profoundly social laws against murder and incest by literalizing the violent ambivalence of identification – the idealizing desire to be like which can so easily slide into the aggressive desire to replace. The dead father is made stronger than the living one by the brothers' deferred and guilty obedience. But, and decisively, he is not only stronger; he is also more loving. The idealization of the symbolic substitute for the father – the totem – represents both an act of obedience and what Freud calls an 'attempt at self-justification' expressed through the following formula: 'If our father had treated us in the way the totem does, we should never have felt tempted to kill him' (*PFL* 13: 206). 'If this murder', Lacan announces in 'On a Question Preliminary to any Possible Treatment of Psychosis', 'is the fruitful moment of debt through which the subject binds himself for life to the Law, the symbolic Father is, insofar as he signifies this Law, the dead Father' (Lacan 1977: 199). Certainly, in 'Totem and Taboo', the 'law' as such, the law as guilt rather than anxiety, can only be instituted over the death of the father. Prior to that moment, the father's desire to control his sons and to keep the women of the group to himself is expressed through an act of exclusion and appropriation which takes place outside of a framework of legality or right – in fact, outside of the familial schema which establishes the relation between 'father' and 'son'. At the same time, in 'Totem and Taboo', Freud continues to stress the retaliatory or vengeful wish aimed at the 'dead' or symbolic father: 'If our father had treated us in the way the totem does.' Better than the 'real' remembered father, the totem carries not only the death and the idealization of the paternal but also its degradation through that wish: if only he had been better . . . The very act of loving the (dead) father, it seems, of symbolizing the loving father through the totem, shames the memory of the figure supposed to be the very source and guarantor of the law.

Freud makes two critical moves here. On the one hand, the fiction of loving paternity institutes a social submission to the incest taboo in the form of a renunciation of the father's women; or desire for the father's women is replaced by a wish to be loved by the father in his symbolic form. On the other hand, the loving paternal law which institutes and underwrites the social circulation of women also sets up the possibility of speculation: '*If* our father . . .' In one sense, it is this conditional or fictional 'if' which really kills the primal father, releasing the brothers into a fraternal alliance governed by the symbolic paternal function. In effect, the difference – the sociality – of that function is produced by its apparent opposition to the memory of the 'real' primal father. At its most simple, then, 'Totem and Taboo' gives us a narrative of release from the persecutory pressure of the real and into the possibility of something else – something which is not, however, easily described as a beyond of the patriarchal father. The gap in the real through which the social appears to open up is, after all, the effect of an alliance between sons of fathers and brothers of brothers – a filial tie between sons and fathers, a fraternal contract between brothers of brothers elaborated through the exchange of women. Freud signals the moment of transition from the primal horde to 'civilization' through that exchange and thus produces the category of the woman as an essential, but somehow empty, object in the process of securing the brothers' release from the father's persecution. To put this another way: running parallel with the woman's different relation to, or, more strongly, exclusion within, a social alliance between brothers of brothers, is her exclusion from the 'as if' through which it is mobilized. By placing her both at the centre of and also somewhere beyond the symbolization which founds the fraternal contract, Freud defines the place occupied by the woman in the social fantasy as the effect of the loss of that structure of fantasy – a loss which could be said to lock the woman into a relation with the paternal real.

There seems to be no other way of speculating about the place of the woman within the terms of Freud's phylogenetic fantasy. 'The vicissitudes of women in these primeval times', he writes in the 'Overview of the Transference Neuroses', 'are especially obscure to us' (Freud 1987: 20). Given his famous insistence on the enigma of women and female sexuality, the obscurity that Freud attaches to both in the myth of social origin is not surprising. But there may be something more than the usual difficulty of women at stake in these lines insofar as they – women – remain beyond the reach not simply of a psychoanalysis which attempts to ground its theory in clinical observation but of the speculation in which Freud was so cautiously, and yet so flagrantly, engaged. He cannot even guess at a story without falling back on the innate bisexuality which would, implicitly, allow the woman to take up her place as a brother within the social contract:

> The vicissitudes of women in these primeval times are especially obscure to us. Thus, conditions of life that we have not recognized may come into consideration. But we are spared the grossest difficulty by observing that we should not forget human bisexuality. Thus women can assume the dispositions acquired by men and bring them to light in themselves.
>
> (ibid.)

In this instance, then, Freud falls back onto bisexuality as a way of circumventing the 'grossest difficulty' of trying to imagine women outside of the familial economy of prohibition and exchange which carries the social tie for psychoanalysis. But while the concept of bisexuality provides a way out of the obscurity introduced by the woman into the process of speculating, of fictionalizing, itself, the capacity for bisexuality is forgotten when it comes to describing the desire of the primal father. Whatever Freud's attention to the complex and fragile construction of sexuality, the father's desire for his women is as beyond question in his text as the persecution of his sons. At the same time as he is examining the importance of bisexuality and the socializing sublimation of homosexuality between the brothers of the primal horde, for example, Freud continues to assert the father's violent appropriation of the woman as self-evident:

> As a reward for his power to safeguard the lives of so many other helpless ones he bestowed upon himself unrestrained dominance over them, and through his personality established the first two tenets that he was himself invulnerable and that his possession of women must not be challenged.
>
> (ibid.: 15)

Thus the omnipotence of the primal father is constantly mediated by, secured through, his absolute right to women, a mediation which suggests that if there is no way of speculating differently about the woman, it is because the rights of Narcissus govern the obscurity which conceals her in Freud's theory. Quite simply, 'vicissitudes' are precisely what cannot be allowed to the woman by this story of a father who castrates his 'sons' in the name of his singular rights to his 'daughters' – rights which can only be challenged by the fraternal alliance. To push the point, and Freud's own Oedipal and familial schema, the paternal prohibition that would make sense of the woman's position in the primal horde inverts what will become the Oedipal law requiring the son to renounce all claim to the father's women. By contrast, there is something like a demand on the daughter that she love no one but the father, that she keep to the paternal real rather than participate in the murderous idealization and symbolization of his function.

To put this slightly differently: as soon as we start to put the woman back into the social tie, it is the perversity of this primal paternity which suddenly shows up. From the point of the woman's disruption of the fictionalizing process – implicit in 'Totem and Taboo', interrupting Freud himself in 'Overview of the Transference Neuroses' – we can, I think, compare Narcissus with the father of the seduction theory who keeps his daughter to himself with such devastating psychical and social effects. It should be said, though, that the perversity of Narcissus does not simply concern an asocial breaching of the law against incest, if only because the murder which founds that law has not yet been committed in the chronology of the myth. The demand made on the woman by the primal father is aimed at keeping her bereft of any object other than himself – bereft, that is, of the fraternal alliance founded on the profoundly socializing and fantasmatic effects of an 'as if'.

Freud is giving us an account, then, of how femininity, and, though differently, the woman, is called upon to support the pathology internal to Narcissus and thus to the social fantasy worked through him. Whether she is occupied by or preoccupied with the father, the sexual difference of the woman threatens to expose the violence and perversity of the social processes which Freud attempts to secure through him. At the same time, though, as if she cannot contain that perversity, the more than anxious demand for love that it generates in – or requires from – the daughter is proliferated across sexual difference, threatening to seduce 'the masses' into a permanent discontent. This is, perhaps, one of the effects of Freud's appeal to the concept of bisexuality as a way out of the difficulty of being a woman in the fraternal alliance. The capacity for identification across sexual difference, the instability of sexual distinctions that such an identification must entail, cannot confine the perversion of the paternal function within the relation between the father and his daughter. Such a proliferation is already hinted at, in fact, in the case history of Elisabeth von R. included in *Studies on Hysteria*. The hysterical daughter of a 'vivacious man of the world', Elisabeth von R., Freud suggests, 'found herself drawn into especially intimate contact with her father . . . who used to say that this daughter of his took the place of a son and a friend with whom he could exchange thoughts' (*PFL* 3: 207). Further, this father

> did not fail to observe that her mental constitution was on that account departing from the ideal which people like to see realized in a girl . . . [H]e often said she would find it hard to get a husband. She was in fact greatly discontented with being a girl.
>
> (ibid.)

Here the issue of the female hysteric's own gender identification, and its perversion, is set alongside the (at least implicit) seductiveness of the father through the case studies. Only a perverse femininity, it seems, can be a son to the father – that is, not only femininity as a perversion of an ideal type of masculinity but a perversion of that perverse femininity itself. In what sense, after all, can the daughter be a (friendly) son, especially to the father, when what produces the category of the son for psychoanalysis is an identification with the paternal function from which Freud explicitly excludes the woman?

Freud's myth of Narcissus, which I will discuss further in the next chapter, can takes its place among the fantasies of origins identified by Laplanche and Pontalis (Laplanche and Pontalis 1964: 19). Just as the primal scene 'pictures' the 'origin of the individual', the fantasy of seduction 'the origin and upsurge of sexuality' and fantasies of castration 'the origin of the difference between the sexes', so the origin of the social tie is presented through the fantasies of the primal Narcissus, a fascination with the love and the death, the seduction and perversion, of the father – fascination which then appears in the public and private fantasies of the social process. This is, I think, Adorno's key insight, set out, elliptically, as we've seen, in 'Transparencies on Film' and more obviously in 'Freudian Theory and the Pattern of Fascist Propaganda' in which he refers to an increasingly influential opinion that 'the specifically fascist leader type does not seem to be a father figure such as for instance the king of former times' (Adorno 1991: 120). The inconsistency of this with Freud's theory of the leader as a rememoration of the primal father is, for Adorno, 'only superficial'. He goes back to Freud's description of identification, in 'Group Psychology and the Analysis of the Ego' (1921), as the earliest form of emotional tie to the other in order to underline the pre-Oedipal elements of group identification and the possibility of a more archaic image behind the authority of the Oedipal father:

> It may well be that this pre-oedipal component of identification helps to bring about the separation of the leader image as that of an all-powerful primal father, from the actual father image. Since the child's identification with his father as an answer to the Oedipus complex is only a secondary phenomenon, infantile regression may go beyond this father image and through an 'anaclitic' process reach a more archaic one.
>
> (ibid.: 120)

Adorno is careful to stress the need for further clarification of these points. But his emphasis on the pathology of the primal father is striking – not least because, in the circulation of terms between psychoanalysis and the Frankfurt School, it starts to articulate the asocial identifications which Freud attributes to women and the masses with the debasement of the paternal function itself. Put this alongside the reading of the culture industry as both a perversion and usurpation of the paternal function and we have an account of the cinema as a type of regressive father – an external and thus simultaneously loving and threatening father – soliciting the dependent forms of identification supposed to constitute the demanding feminine superego for Freud. Think back, too, to Modleski's critique of the female spectator who is 'deeply touched', even dazzled, by the loving paternity she sees on screen (Modleski 1988: 80). That dazzling, its potential for preoccupation of the woman, starts to articulate the category of the female spectator with the psycho-analytic category of the feminine superego insofar as the woman/daughter responds to the screen – more or less melancholically, more or less desperately, perhaps – with something like a demand to be loved.

There is no obvious sense, then, in which the female spectator – and the mass spectator for whom, in this instance, she stands as a prototype – can simply welcome what, in 1975, Mulvey described as a 'decline of the traditional film form' (Mulvey 1975: 33). There is something involuntary behind the fascination with the mass or masculine fantasies of cinema, something which goes beyond an identification, pleasurable or not, through recognition with what is taking place on screen, something that can be used to examine the mass-feminine axis uncovered through a dialogue between feminist, psychoanalytic and critical theories of film. I want to conclude this chapter by returning, briefly, both to the vilified spectators of John Hughes's films and to the family romance between brother and sister through which I started to examine the form of spectatorship which seemed to be proposed by the final frames of *Ferris Bueller's Day Off*. There is, I've suggested, a decisive and mistaken look required by the end of the film from a spectator who stays too long and asks too much from the fantasy displayed on screen. It is tempting to see the film's final prohibition – 'Go home. Go!' – as proof of Adorno's thesis that cinema works as a form of social superego. If this is the case, then our spectator is only too obviously and massively overwhelmed by a feminine identification with the cinema-father by whom she, or he, demands to be loved. But it is, of course, no accident that the spectator finds herself in the awkward position of having violated a cinematic sense of an ending. The credits for *Ferris Bueller's Day Off* come up before the end of the film, before the narrative which tells how Ferris, with the help of his now loving sister, finally ruins the overbearing and vindictive authority of the school principal, Rooney. Rooney's ride home on the school bus keeps the spectator watching so that she is there when Ferris comes back on screen to point out that she has been lured into asking for what she cannot possibly have. (It is difficult not to be reminded of the little girl's response to the sight of the boy's penis: 'She has seen it and knows that she is without it and wants to have it' (*PFL* 7:

336).)[3] The persistent and displaced demand to be loved, then, is intimately bound up with a previous 'seduction', with the film's insistence that we stay and watch – and wait.

Thus beyond the narrative and images *shown* on the screen, this cinema seems able to mobilize identifications that, following Freud, we would have to describe not simply as masculine or feminine but as filial and superegoic. What is perhaps most interesting about Hughes's cinema in this context is the general critical agreement that his 'teen' films demote, even devastate, the paternal function. The fathers are not *visible*. Thomas Doherty, for example, describes the contemporary teenager on film as dispossessed of rebellious protest by a parent culture which assumes neither authority nor omnipotence:

> Up against a parent culture that is ever more accommodating and appeasing, ever less authoritative and overbearing (not to mention present), the teenage rebel faces a problem the Wild One never anticipated. The parental and principal villains in teenpics like *Risky Business* or *Ferris Bueller's Day Off* are overdrawn caricatures, no real threat, played for laughs. One of the most fascinating undertones of teenpics since the 1960s is their palpable desire for parental control and authority, not adolescent independence and freedom.
>
> (Doherty 1988: 157)

Doherty's reading of contemporary youth cinema as dominated by a historically new desire to relocate the paternal, or parental, function (and we can compare Modleski here) is complicated by the film which has become a standard cinematic reference point for adolescent rebellion. In Nicholas Ray's *Rebel Without a Cause* (1955) there is also a 'palpable desire' for paternal authority, and the alternative family set up by the adolescent rebel, Jimmy (James Dean), can be described as simultaneously an attack upon, and a demand made to, a paternity which is failing through the father who refuses either to 'stand up' to the domineering mother or for his son. Jimmy's effort to establish an alternative family with Judy and Plato is as much an attempt to put the emasculated father back into a position of authority over his wife and son as it is an investment in peer group solidarity as source of refuge from a persecutory, or alienating, parental culture. The ambivalence of this double aim in the prototypical 'rebel film', then, tends to recast Doherty's historical differentiation between the 1960s and the 1980s in terms of a new desire for the father as a symptom of mourning for figures of authoritative opposition to 'the Establishment'. The critical force of this mourning – if it is that – is its attention to the need for historical, cultural and political distinctions between mainstream films – films which can be so easily run together and dismissed. At the same time, it highlights a disjuncture between the easy wish fulfilment so frequently associated with the 'clean pics' and the discontent, or, more strongly, the persecutory affect, they can generate within a film criticism that seems almost to lament cinema's refusal to establish a sufficiently persecuting authority.

But the critical theories discussed in both this and the previous chapter suggest that the lack of an *image* of, or narrative function assigned to, the father does not amount to the absence of the paternal from cinema. *Ferris* can stand as an example of a cinema which represents youth rebellion as nothing more than a series of tricks, as a revelling in parental wealth and status which typifies the hedonism of an 'I want it now' generation. But one of the film's most ambiguous jokes depends on a type of relocation of the paternal in the figure of the adolescent male. Briefly, the day out, and Ferris's narrative omnipotence, depend on his being able to outwit the authorities and get his girlfriend out of school. To do this, he pretends there has been a death in Sloan's family and masquerades as her father. Under the gaze of the school principal, Rooney, Ferris waits for Sloan at the entrance to the school and asks her for the kiss that could be described as the symptom of the paternity invested by the film: 'Do you have a kiss for daddy?' Rooney's look registers this exchange as both incestuous and perverse – 'So that's how it is in their family?' – his surprised indifference used to draw attention to the incestuous play which structures the joke. Inflected as adolescent rebelliousness, the kiss between Sloan and her boyfriend/father is framed first by the spectator's look that denies its perversity because 'we know' that Ferris is not really the father he is pretending to be and then by Rooney's 'mistaken' look – a look which finds, by misrecognizing, perversity.

Tentatively, this brief and clichéd exchange insists on parading, as a joke, the perverse paternal function which is said to be embedded both in the film narratives and the structure of spectatorship and identification of (mass) cinema as such – as if Hughes's cinema is staging, or enacting, the accusation being made against it. The perversity in the request, or demand, for a kiss is simultaneously displayed and concealed by the image of the male adolescent so that the film can behave like Narcissus, requiring that the spectator/ daughter give up the pleasures of the fantasmatic 'as if', of wishing to be like or, as Kluge might put it, of critical fantasy, and devote herself to demanding love from him. This may be the source of the persecutory affect associated with cinema as a mass phenomenon, with cinema as a death threat to oppositional fantasy, or, finally, to fantasy as such. If so, then it is a threat which, like Freud's daughters, the spectator is asked to take on as the effect of her own foolish and melancholic demand for love.

Chapter 4

Rumble Fish

Francis Coppola, Susan Hinton and Narcissus

I looked on all the world as if it were populated by brothers alone
. . . Yet it is striking that in spite of having such brothers, whose
sister I am still today proud and happy to be . . . I was nevertheless
miserably lonely with all of them and closely devoted to my
fantasy life as my only joy.

(Lou Andreas-Salomé, *The Freud Journal*)

Accompanying the black and white photograph of the author on the
inside front cover of the TeenTracks edition of *Rumble Fish*, there
is a short, but intriguing, biography:

'I never set out to be a ground breaker or to be controversial. I just
wanted to tell the truth about teenage life and to tell it the way it
really is. Most adults don't remember, or don't want to remember,
the emotional intensity and the idealism of being a teenager.
That's what makes my work different. Mostly I just remember real
well what it was like to be a teenager. Some of the problems
change, but the feelings don't.'

S.E. Hinton's first novel, *The Outsiders*, was published when she
was seventeen. She was born in Tulsa, in America, where she still
lives with her husband and son Nicholas.

(Hinton 1977)

The first thing to notice about these now famous adolescent imaginaries of male bonding, then, is that they are written by a young
woman. *Rumble Fish* was first published in the UK in 1976 but, as
the copyright information makes clear, extracts from the novel first
appeared in the University of Tulsa Alumni Magazine in 1968, while
Hinton was still in her teens. Hinton went on to work with Francis
Coppola on the screen play of *Rumble Fish*, shot back to back with

The Outsiders in Tulsa, Oklahoma in 1983. She also appeared briefly in both films – in *The Outsiders* as a nurse, and *Rumble Fish* as a prostitute.

There is, I think, a felt disjuncture between what is described on the back cover of *Rumble Fish* as 'the violent ganglands of urban America' which Hinton presents through her stories and the woman-liness that is so carefully attached to her biography and image. Apparently posing for a family 'snapshot' with two small dogs, the visual coding of Hinton as both domestic and maternal (which dispels the ambiguity of that 'S.E.' even though her full name, Susan, does not appear on the cover of the book) is reinforced by the description of her as a wife and a mother (of a son), as a woman who doesn't go away, who stays where she is and who 'still lives' in Tulsa. A type of banality is structuring the public image of Hinton – a banality which is in stunning contrast not only to the seductive masculinity displayed in the films but also, and perhaps symptom-atically, to the unsettling effects introduced by a woman who could be said to have found a way to write herself into the place of the brother. Hinton's use of first-person male narrators, Rusty-James in *Rumble Fish*, Ponyboy Curtis in *The Outsiders*, reinforces the disturbing presence of a woman who does not only represent masculinity but seems almost to usurp or to inhabit it, to take masculinity as her mask:

> I sucked in my gut and wrapped the chain around his neck, jerking him to the ground. All I wanted to do was get the knife away from him. I'd kill him later.
>
> (Hinton 1977: 22)

> That afternoon turned out to be more interesting than I'd bargained for, I got expelled, and Patty broke up with me.
>
> (ibid.: 46)

> I was so glad the Motorcycle Boy came home. He was the coolest person in the whole world. Even if he hadn't been my brother he would have been the coolest person in the whole world. And I was going to be just like him.
>
> (ibid.: 31)

Whether it is describing a knife fight, the loss of a girlfriend or, most unstably, the desire to be like a brother, the 'I' of *Rumble Fish* is inevitably caught up in an identification across sexual difference which very quickly implicates Hinton in a writing of masculinity that must – because she is a woman – fail. In an article published in *Monthly Film Bulletin* to coincide with the release of *The Outsiders*, Cynthia Rose points to Hinton's misrepresentation of masculinity as the key failure of her work. 'Hinton claims', Rose comments, 'that she began *The Outsiders* to see if she could construct . . . "a world outside the narrow confines of school, with no parents or authority figures . . . a place where kids live by their own rules"' (Rose 1983: 238). The use of 'claims' here sounds the note of suspicion in Rose's assessment of Hinton, a suspicion which derives from her conviction that as 'a woman imagining how young men feel, speak and interact', Hinton is getting it wrong:

> [H]er heroes sometimes err on the side of over-sensitivity and poetic perception. (Ponyboy's spontaneous recitation of an entire Robert Frost poem to Johnny in *The Outsiders* and the Motorcycle Boy's stilted self-explications in *Rumble Fish* are two outstanding examples.) A more unsettling characteristic is the machismo lavished on all the male characters at the expense both of natural adolescent awkwardness and of their female counterparts.
>
> (ibid.)

Rose adds a class dimension to this when she notes that Hinton is from a 'middle-class rather than a sub-blue collar background' described in her narratives. That is, Hinton is said to be writing beyond both her sex and her class, but the class discrepancy does not function as the limit point of the 'realistic', as opposed to the 'stylized', novel. On the contrary, Rose praises Hinton's 'characterisation of the emotional claustrophobia and relentlessly limited prospects of the poor white world – where sacrifice so often defines love' as her 'most impressive literary achievement' (ibid.). Only when sex and class coincide is that achievement compromised by Hinton's tendency to lavish machismo on her male characters while ignoring her women or girls, a tendency Rose links to the influence of Jim Carroll's *The Basketball Diaries*, first published in 1963 and described as an 'even bigger-selling youth success than Hinton's books'.[1] Thus Rose's discussion of the differences between Hinton and Carroll sets out forcefully an association between sexual difference and narrative knowledge; or, more precisely, Rose underlines the act of representing the other sex as one that immediately puts narrative knowledge, and with it literary realism, into question. The machismo of Carroll's *Diaries*, she suggests, is genuine because 'their author is a reformed junkie and street hustler writing from personal experience'. By contrast, Hinton is just a middle-class young woman who used the money she earned from *The Outsiders* to 'major in education at the University of Tulsa, where she met her husband and made the decision to take up teaching' (ibid.). Once again, at least in comparison to being a real reformed junkie and hustler, a certain banality is making itself felt in the story told about Hinton – the banality which is, it seems, indissociable from being a woman: 'More to the point, perhaps, is his [Carroll's] sex – from a man, street macho and street slang issue with a different authority and resonance' (ibid.: 239). Even more than his experience of the street, then, it is Carroll's sex which guarantees the realism, the sexual reality, of his writing. Hinton's sex, her identification as a woman, dispossesses her writing of its claim to 'tell it the way it is', turning her work into an illegitimate appropriation of masculine identity which can only be perverted by its passing through the woman, by a writing which errs both on the side of a feminine 'over-sensitivity' and a 'more unsettling' masculine machismo. Thus there seems to be too much sexedness in play in Hinton's work, too much masculinity and femininity and all of it in the wrong place – a sexual displacement which, Rose insists, leads her to lose sight of both narrative realism and the woman.

Rose's critique is, I think, governed by a reproach to Hinton which owes something to a feminist demand on the female author to write for and about *women*. If Rose is uncomfortable with Hinton's writing beyond her 'experience', the other side of the discomfort is a wish that she would write what she does 'know' about being a young woman. That wish, in turn, supports the questions which, while never made explicit, structure Rose's argument: why does a woman choose to write about young men and then claim to do so in the name of a memory of what it was really like? What is the status of that remembering if what takes place in the novels has nothing to do with a real memory that could be claimed by the woman and everything to do with 'adolescent wish-fulfilment' (ibid.: 238)? In short, what is the woman's desire in these imaginaries of 'illusory group identity', these 'ultra-romantic imposition[s] of the gang myth' on to small-town America (ibid.: 239)?

The first difficulty is knowing how to question the relation between femininity and fantasy in the sexual and social identifica-tions represented through Hinton's work without recourse to a psycho-biography of Hinton which would then have to claim her as a type of representative of women's fantasmatic and desiring relation to the masculine and collective identities of her novels. Crudely, then, even before the complication introduced by Coppola's film-making, there is a problem about how to read Hinton's text. That problem reinflects Kaja Silverman's subtle rereading of Freud's 'A Child is Being Beaten' in which the female subject represents herself as the 'ambiguous spectator' of a group of passive boys: 'Some boys are being beaten. [I am probably looking on.]' Freud, as Silverman shows, ignores the 'burning question', embedded in this formulation, 'of what it might mean, *apart from simple disguise*, for a female subject to represent herself in phantasy as a group of passive boys' (Silverman 1988: 49; my italics). In effect, Silverman goes on to suggest, the position of the female spectator in this form of masochistic fantasy – if that is what it is – amounts to an 'unthinkable' (for the woman) identification with a passive male homo-sexuality which works to redefine male subjectivity away from its association with both agency and aggression (ibid.: 50). Unlike the female spectator of the beating fantasy, however, Hinton does not seem to be engaged in a redefinition of masculinity and/as maso-chism. On the contrary, what is perhaps most striking about her fiction is its mismatch between sexual and social identification: between the feminine sexual identification ascribed to Hinton and the gender identification of her writing which usurps both the *sex* of masculinity and its privileged *social* instance through the bond between brothers. In this sense, Rose's unease with Hinton's project has to do with the way in which, via an identification across sexual difference, the woman may occupy the fictionalizing and socializing place of the brother without, apparently, questioning the privileging of that place.

That sexual mismatch and its gendering of the social bond suggest the purchase of a psychoanalytic account of the sexual difference of identification in approaching Hinton's fiction – in particular, the juncture between that fiction and Coppola's film. More precisely, it is the concept of masquerade which clamours for attention – not least because it has been so central to a feminism which turns to psychoanalysis for an account of the way in which the category of the woman and the category of femininity are as inadequate to one another as they are necessary. First published in *The International Journal of Psychoanalysis* in 1929, Joan Rivière's 'Womanliness as a Masquerade' has also been central to recent debates about film, femininity and the image of the woman.[2] Rivière used the concept of masquerade to describe her patient, a successful, 'intellectual' woman who suffered from an anxious compulsion to seek reassurance and attention from men 'at the close of proceedings in which she had taken part or been the principal figure' (Rivière 1986: 36). She linked the woman's compulsive behaviour to her wish to 'hide the possession of masculinity' – conventionally associated with the woman's academic success and public performance – and so to 'avert the reprisal expected if she was found to possess it' (ibid.: 38). At first sight, the conventional demarcation of (public) masculinity and (passive) femininity in Rivière's analysis does not seem to offer much to a feminist reading. But that convention is qualified by the famous and ambiguous statement at the centre of the paper which governs what is being said about a 'womanliness' which can be 'assumed and worn as a mask' but which is no less genuine for that:

> The reader may now ask how I define womanliness or where I draw the line between genuine womanliness and the 'masquerade'. My suggestion is not, however, that there is any such difference; whether radical or superficial, they are the same thing. The capacity for womanliness was there in this woman . . . but . . . was used far more as a device for avoiding anxiety than as a primary mode of sexual enjoyment.
>
> (ibid.)

At this point, both psychoanalysis and feminism encounter a similar difficulty embedded in a theoretical oscillation between a constitutional or essential sexuality which is always, in the last instance, in place (or at least able to be put in its place) and a way of thinking about identity as that which evades recovery or completion – as a permanent work-in-progress which puts any adequacy between the woman and her femininity into question. There is an enormous tension between a womanliness that, like the clothing to which it is so frequently compared, can be put on or off like a mask and femininity as a capacity, or primary mode of being (sexual) for the woman – a tension that Rivière does not resolve and which can sustain two quite different, though sometimes inseparable, appropriations of the concept of masquerade. As the effect of an alienation imposed on women by the demand that they participate in a masculine or patriarchal structure of desire which represses an authentic femininity, the visual convention of the masquerade suggests an ultimately recoverable and knowable essence of the feminine. But, by contrast, as a spectacle of sexual oscillation and pretence, the masquerade becomes the distinguishing feature of a femininity equated with non-identity as such, a femininity which speaks the impossibility of finally achieving, or knowing, the identity of either sex, male or female.

The very real difficulty of this opposition has tended to over-shadow an essential aspect of Rivière's argument – specifically, the link between the masquerade and the woman's more or less guilty representation of masculinity.[3] Rivière herself does not make very much of this but it is clear that her patient assumes a mask of womanliness only after she has represented herself as a man by undertaking the kind of work and performance associated with the public sphere of men. The masquerade, then, is staged after mascul-inity has been performed by a woman – and a spectacle of femininity is called upon to mitigate the effects of a prior spectacle of masculinity. This convention of femininity is taken on to assuage an anxiety which has two different sources and takes two different forms. First, the woman makes a demand for direct reassurance about her performance – she wants, Rivière suggests, to be assured that she has done nothing 'inappropriate'. Second, more importantly, we're told, she wants 'indirect reassurance of the nature of sexual atten-tions from these men' (ibid.: 36). The woman wants a sexual encounter with the men she singles out as able to give her the reassurance she craves. To put this slightly differently: she wants to know both that she has performed appropriately for the masculinity she has usurped – even though, for the Oedipal schema that Rivière uses to explain her patient's unconscious fantasy life, a successful performance is itself proof that she is in possession of the father's penis – and that her successful display is not going to provoke reprisals from these men. In this sense, proof of her sexual attrac-tiveness is proof that men aren't angry even though she may be guilty. Even though she may be in possession of the father's penis, she is still a woman in relation to the men in the audience.

No doubt the incompatibility of these demands contributes to the way in which the very act of making such an appeal turns the woman's performance into a failure. However successful her repre-sentation of masculinity has been, she lets the side down im-mediately afterwards by indulging in a 'compulsive ogling and coquetting' which, however veiled, constitutes a sexual advance (ibid.: 37). Her fault, then, is not, or not only, that she has stolen her father's penis and pretended to be a man but that she has not pretended well enough. The woman's masquerade inevitably bears fatal traces of her femininity as both a defence against and an advance towards men and her appropriation of masculinity betrays itself by making known its fear of, as well as its desire for, a man. Further, if masculinity can be usurped then its genuineness, *its* essential nature, is at once put into question – a question which, in this case, cannot be kept apart from the homosexual desire implicit in the 'masculine' woman's overtures to her male spectators.

Reading across from Joan Rivière to Cynthia Rose, the sexuality, the sexual authenticity, of masculinity is at risk from the moment the woman attempts to represent it – a risk that, for Rose at least, seems immediately to generate a type of prohibition against the woman's representation of sexual difference. As we've already seen, Rose's appeal to literary realism suggests that if Hinton gets masculinity wrong then she would do better to write something else: sexual difference and a realist aesthetic combine to restrict the woman's access to a fictional 'as if' precisely when she tries to imagine masculinity and an invested form of masculine collective identity. Inevitably, this critical response to Hinton recalls, or more strongly, seems to repeat, Freud's gesture of exclusion of the woman from the speculative and conditional 'if our father had . . .' which, as we've seen, institutes the fraternal alliance – as if something has to put a brake on the woman's fantasy of that alliance, albeit in the name of a proper representation of the woman.

There is a sense in which the woman's access to fiction, or to fantasy, becomes intimately bound up with her access to the social tie at this point. And in this sense, again, the image and the writing of S.E. Hinton seem both to confirm and to unsettle what Sheila Johnston has described as the forcible expulsion of the 'female Other' in her reviews of Coppola's *The Outsiders* and *Rumble Fish* – shot back to back in 1983. *The Outsiders* was dedicated to the librarian and students of the Lone Star Junior High School, Fresno, California, who had written to Coppola asking him to make a film out of their favourite book. Coppola agreed. 'I wanted to make a movie about youth, and about belonging', he has said, 'belonging to a group of people with whom you made identification, and where you felt real love. Even though those boys were poor and, in a way, insignificant, the story gives them a kind of beauty and nobility' (Coppola, quoted by Adair 1983: 287). 'Those boys', the 'Greasers', are the working-class boys with whom, for most reviewers of the film, Coppola was clearly identifying (Adair 1983; Corliss 1983a; Ansen 1983). The gang is the group towards which the variously orphaned or abandoned boys gravitate, the site of a relation between brothers in both senses: the family of brothers (Darrel, Sodapop and Ponyboy Curtis) and the fraternal alliance set up between members of the group. The film begins and ends with 14-year-old Ponyboy Curtis writing a school essay on the rivalry between the wealthy 'Socs' and the Greasers, a rivalry which culminates in the death of a Soc, killed in self-defence by Ponyboy's best friend, Johnny. With the help of another Greaser, Dallas, Johnny and Ponyboy go into hiding out of town until Johnny hears that the Soc's girlfriend will testify in his defence and decides to stand trial. On the way home, Johnny is badly injured when he, Ponyboy and Dallas rescue some children from a burning church – the adults in charge of the kids failing to do anything – and the three of them return to town as 'hoods turned heroes'. A 'rumble' between the Socs and the Greasers – the film's set-piece as a gang film – is organized in Johnny's honour but he dies in hospital soon afterwards. His death sends Dallas over the edge. Brandishing an empty gun, he holds up a general store and is shot dead by the police just as the gang arrives.

Shot in Panavision, *The Outsiders* is almost invariably yoked to *Gone with the Wind* – for its 'sunset vistas' and 'romantic melancholia' (Johnston 1983: 237) – and to *Rebel Without a Cause* for its sympathetic representation of the 'juvenile delinquent'. It is also famous for its images of male beauty. 'Seldom', notes Gilbert Adair, 'has film camera lingered so amorously on the tiny highlight of a satiny lower lip and the soft liquidity of an adolescent's eyes. *The Outsiders* verges on the homo-erotic' (Adair 1983: 287). Richard Corliss links that homo-eroticism directly to the film's investment in male bonding as 'familial, embracing, unself-consciously homo-erotic . . . Their ideal world is both a womb and a locker room: no women need apply to this dreamy brotherhood' (Corliss 1983a: 78).

This possibly overly familiar link between a homo-eroticized form of social identification and a repudiation of femininity runs through reviews of *The Outsiders*. 'There is a careless homoeroticism about this peer group', Sheila Johnston argues, ' – climaxing in the ecstatic "rumble" in a downpour of rain – that can effectively dispense with the presence of women' (Johnston 1983: 237). Thus a more or less repressed, a 'careless' or 'unself-conscious', homosexual desire is consistently invoked as an explanation both for the flagrant masculine beauty on display through the film and for the intensity of the identificatory ties between the members of the gang – ties underlined by the exclusion of the woman. In effect, these readings are turning Coppola's description of *The Outsiders* around. Instead of being

about 'making identification' and 'feeling real love', the film
becomes the expression of a desire to 'make real love' under the
guise of 'feeling identification'. In other words, *The Outsiders*
becomes a symptom of masculine desire for itself mirrored in and
through the image of an other who is always the beautiful same.

As if to stress the fraternal bond between the films themselves, the
critical emphasis on an eroticized homosociality is carried over to
the readings of *Rumble Fish*. Chris Auty, who otherwise stresses the
differences between the two films, finds its 'substance' in the 'heavy-
lidded lyricism of the two boys' fantasies, charmed by their own
physical beauty' (Auty 1984: 152) and, as we've seen, Sheila
Johnston insists that the film's scenario is one that

> forcibly expels the female Other. The absent mother is supplanted
> by the Motorcycle Boy who exactly resembles her, just as his
> brother jealously lures him away from Cassandra, just as Rusty-
> James rejects his girl for peer-group solidarity . . . the impatiently
> waiting gang.
>
> (Johnston 1984: 8)

At the same time, *Rumble Fish* is seen as the 'problem' or delinquent
film of the pair, the film that doesn't quite work as a gang myth. It
revises the themes of its companion film '*en noir*', Johnston
continues, and the rumble fish of the title suggest not gang warfare
but 'an aggression directed, as if by some demented Narcissus,
against one's image seen in a glass' (ibid.). Writing for *Time*
magazine, Richard Corliss described the film as Coppola's 'suicide
note' to the film industry, as 'baroque', 'self-indulgent' and 'brave'
(Corliss 1983b: 91). None of the 'dead souls' on screen, he suggests,

> ever enters the land of living drama, where obsession and ambigu-
> ity intersect and a poor soul in the dark can look up at a figure on
> the screen and say, 'Hey, that's me.' Instead, one suspects,
> Coppola wants the moviegoer to shout, 'Hey, what's *that*?'.
>
> (ibid.)

Rumble Fish could, perhaps, be described as the gang film that
never was. The gangs are fragile, even delusive, memories against
which the relation between Rusty-James (Matt Dillon) and his elder
brother, the Motorcycle Boy (Mickey Rourke), is played out.
Recalling the idealizing and aggressive logic of identification
analysed by Mikkel Borch-Jacobsen ('I want what my brother, my
model, my idol wants: and I want it in his place' (Borch-Jacobsen

1989: 27)), Rusty-James's desire to be like the Motorcycle Boy runs through the film – 'When I'm older I'm going to be just like him, I'm going to look like him' – even in the face of an insistence that 'you're never gonna be like that, man'. It is Rusty-James who, in his brother's absence, carries on the myth of the gangs the Motorcycle Boy once led. Even when he returns, apparently from a bike trip to California, the Motorcycle Boy shows no interest in reviving the gangs or in 'running this side of town'. Instead he becomes obsessed with the 'rumble fish' in a local pet store, an obsession which makes Rusty-James doubt his sanity and brings to a head what seems to be a long-running conflict between the Motorcycle Boy and a local police officer, Patterson. Rusty-James is unable to keep his brother from breaking into the store and setting the caged animals free. Telling Rusty-James to get on a motorcycle and go 'clear to the ocean', the Motorcycle Boy starts to take the fish to the river and is shot dead by Patterson. Rusty-James is left to put the fish in the river and, escaping from the police, steals a motorcycle and rides off – his shadow moving across the graffiti which punctuates the film: 'The Motorcycle Boy Reigns.'

A sense of *Rumble Fish* as a difficult film has to do with the way in which it seems to disrupt generic codes, a disruption which is immediately felt in any attempt to give a summary of the film's 'plot'. One reviewer pointed to a mismatch between the film's 'style' and its 'content' – a mismatch that, once again, turns into a problem of spectatorship. In this case, the problem presented by *Rumble Fish* is how to watch a 'teen violence' film that looks like an 'art' movie, a gang film which, in Coppola's own terms, can be understood as 'Camus for kids':

> Coppola's recent viewing seems to have been German silent films of the '20s, so he has decided to coat the whole enterprise in a startling Expressionist style which is very arresting but hardly appropriate to the matter in hand. As with *The Outsiders*, it's very hard to picture the audience at which the film is aimed.
> (Peachment 1989: 512)

At issue, then, is a loss of distinction between 'high' and 'low' culture – a loss that takes place in and through the film itself, disturbing another conventional, and tenacious, distinction between the aesthetics of avant-garde or marginal cinema and those of mainstream film. As I suggested in Chapter 2, that opposition is, in turn, only too easily mapped onto the difference between a critical and a mass spectatorship. What makes *Rumble Fish* a key film in this context is the way in which, by disturbing the boundaries between a high cultural aesthetic and the teen violence film, it situates itself as neither avant-garde nor mainstream but 'cult' – a term which, however difficult to define, has been consistently attached to the film. When it was first shown on British television in 1988 in a double bill with *The Outsiders*, for example, *Rumble Fish* was introduced as a 'cult classic' by Julien Temple, most famous perhaps for his 'exposé' of Malcolm McLaren and the Sex Pistols, *The Great Rock'n'Roll Swindle* (1979). Temple's role as mediator between Coppola's film and its British television audience itself suggests something about one of the contexts for the film's reception and the type of self-confirmation which makes the category of the cult film at once so obvious and so elusive: a 'cult' film director transfers his cult status to the film he introduces or, more accurately, endorses. It is also worth noting that the films were scheduled to be shown on BBC2 – hence also coded as both 'serious' and 'aesthetic' (worth situating as part of a film 'season' and as an important director's work).

The film's cult status is also invested as a site of (youth) subcultural identification and opposition – the cult film as the place to look for resistance to Hollywood cinema (even if it happens to be a Hollywood film) and the cultural and political conformity associated with it. I will come back to the complexities of this investment in one key reading of *Rumble Fish* as a bike movie. For now, I want just to suggest that the cult film seems to work as a borderline category, existing between and sometimes being collapsed into types of cinema that have somehow managed to establish their differences more securely. As a borderline film, *Rumble Fish* is caught up in a process of transmission of iconography and image both inside and outside of cinema. That transmission starts to break down the opposition between the high cultural stylistics 'coating' the film's knife fights – its black and white surrealism, for example, or its distorted, 'Expressionist' camera angles – and its 'stupid' no one and nowhere characters. In fact, the critical insistence on Rusty-James's futile simple-mindedness is remarkable (and it echoes the disrespect we've seen demonstrated for the spectators of another kind of teen film): 'His [the Motorcycle Boy's] kid brother (Dillon) idolises him, but is too stupid to see the damage done to all concerned by the continuous gang-fights of frightful violence but no importance' (Peachment 1989: 512); 'It is not given to his [Coppola's] "hero", incorrigibly stupid, to seek escape through learning' (Johnston 1984:

8). It is the same critical response which, by stressing a disjuncture between the visuality of *Rumble Fish* and its 'story', treats the film itself as a type of masquerade that loses its audience because it slides between two hermetically sealed domains: a European aesthetic tradition and a disaffected or delinquent teen culture. But what gets overlooked here is the process of visual citation which transports images between – and makes them familiar, or, more strongly, welcome to – otherwise disparate and distant sites of cultural identification. The aesthetics of *Rumble Fish* are very much a case in point here. To take just one example: we can see this process of transmission working through the film's debt to German Expressionist cinema, specifically to Robert Wiene's *The Cabinet of Dr. Caligari* (1919), noted for its annulling of 'conventional aspect by means of painted shadows in disharmony with the lighting effects, and zigzag delineations designed to efface all rules of perspective' (Kracauer 1972: 14). The image of Cesare, the somnambulist in *Caligari*, its 'disharmony' and 'effacement', were made famous in 1979 when the 'indie' band Bauhaus used a production still from the film to market their first EP, *Bela Lugosi's Dead* (see frontispiece).[4] The black and white image of Cesare carrying a dead or unconscious woman (it is not clear which from the still itself) draped over his arm took off as a visual and cultural reference point for a 'goth underground' (underlined by Bauhaus's performance of the song in the opening sequence of Tony Scott's *The Hunger*, also released in 1983) that precisely confirms, or reinforces, an association between the visual landscape passing between *Caligari* and *Rumble Fish* and a youth culture embroiled in the seduction exercised by images of stylized violence.

It is this kind of exchange which signals the status of *Rumble Fish* as a cult film and its visuality as neither inappropriate nor surprising but familiar.[5] It is in this sense, too, that the difficulty of imagining or 'picturing' the spectator for the film has to be understood as a problem that goes beyond any (mis)appropriation of a high cultural aesthetic in the name of a romanticized 'ennobling' of working-class punks or disaffected youths. Insofar as *Rumble Fish* does find and/or construct its audience, its bewildered or lost spectators start to tell us something different about the strategies of spectatorship and identification provoked by, or brought to, the film. The first point to be made here is that it is as if the identification so often called upon to make sense of *The Outsiders* is complicated by *Rumble Fish*, a complication that affects both Coppola's (or the narratives of

Coppola's) identification with the film and the identifications between spectator and screen. On the one hand, Coppola's own
flamboyant status as Hollywood's rebellious outsider is read by
reviewers as a reinflected wish that aims not so much at the
construction of an alternative to mainstream Hollywood production
– Coppola's Zoetrope Studio venture – but at the destruction of
belonging as such (*Rumble Fish* as Coppola's death wish or suicide
note). On the other hand, that disaffection is then passed on to the
spectator as confusion, as a failure of recognition which transforms
the illusory identification of 'that's me' into the bewilderment of
'what's that?'.

We can perhaps start to clarify this by turning the argument around
and looking at what happens when *Rumble Fish* is read as a film that,
rather than disrupting or disturbing the process of identification,
confirms it; that is, when it is read as a film which invests cinema as
site of social identifications through its enigmatic and idealized
leader, the Motorcycle Boy. In 'Francis Coppola and the Crisis of
Patriarchy', a section of a chapter on 'crisis' films in *Camera
Politica* (1990), Michael Ryan and Douglas Kellner make a link
between the representation of brotherhood and male bonding in
Coppola's films, from *You're A Big Boy Now* (1967), through *The
Godfather* (1972) to *The Outsiders* and *Rumble Fish*, and what they
describe as a 'conservative turn in the popular imaginary' (Ryan and
Kellner 1990: 49). Like so many critics of 1980s cinema, Ryan and
Kellner start from the sense that something has changed between the
1960s and the 1980s, something that has to do with a reactionary
backlash against the disturbance introduced across the range of socio-
political and cultural spheres by the civil rights movements of the
1960s and 1970s. That disturbance, they suggest, finds expression in
a regressive desire for authority, for 'compensatory models of
redemptive leadership' which can contain the 'broadly felt popular
fantasies and fears' generated by the different challenges to various
social and political institutions: the family, capitalism, democracy,
racism, sexism, heterosexuality (ibid.: 51). Ryan and Kellner locate
the new conservatism as a defensive response to an anxiety which is
both 'real' (economic recession) and 'imaginary' (an attachment to,
and revival of, traditional social models in the face of the discontent
mobilized by economic insecurity).

While the authors' attention to what could be called the real event
of economic crisis is essential, it brings with it the problem of the
relation between base and superstructure, between the real and the

ideological or imaginary – a problem presented here as one of
theorizing the relation between social history and cinematic representation: 'An understanding of the ideology of contemporary
Hollywood film is therefore inseparable from the social history of
the era' (ibid.: 7). For Ryan and Kellner, not all Hollywood films are
'inherently ideological' and there are 'necessary distinctions between different films at different moments of history' (ibid.: 1). But,
in a way that is curiously reminiscent of Alexander Kluge's approach
to the work of fantasy in mainstream film, the possibility of a non-
or anti-ideological cinema reduces the categories of fantasy and of
ideology to defence. Emphasizing the need to revise a traditional
Marxist framework for understanding ideology as 'the system of
ideals and images which operates to enlist the oppressed in their own
subjugation – control without the exercise of force' (ibid.: 14), Ryan
and Kellner propose a model of ideology as a system of cultural
representations which 'like mental representations in relation to the
psyche, orient thought and behavior in a manner that maintains order
and establishes boundaries on proper action':

> Rather than conceive of ideology as a simple exercise in domin-
> ation, we suggest that it be conceived of as a response to forces
> which, if they were not pacified, would tear the social system
> asunder from inside. Indeed, one could say that the very necessity
> of ideology testifies to something amiss within society, since a
> society that was not threatened would not need ideological
> defenses. By attempting to pacify, channel, and neutralize the
> forces that would invert the social system of inequality were they
> not controlled, ideology testifies to the power of those forces . . .
> By reacting against the structural tensions and potentially dis-
> ruptive forces of an inegalitarian society in a way that attempts
> to render them invisible, film ideology must also simultaneously
> put them on display – just as excessively washed hands testify to
> offstage guilt, or as abundance of white blood cells points to
> disease.
>
> (ibid.: 14)

It may be because they dismiss Althusserian Marxism for a simp-
listic condemnation of the individual as a 'political category' that
Ryan and Kellner are able to slide over the complexity of Marxist
theorizations of ideology (ibid.: 274).[6] More immediately relevant
here, however, is the way in which, via the parallel set up between
socio-cultural and psychical forms of representation, the 'forces'

threatening to break through the ideological defences mobilized by the dominant social order seem to be more or less assimilable to the order, or disorder, of biological instinct. The white blood cells 'defending' against disease suggest an instinct for (self-)preservation that, in the logic of this analogy, underlies the resistance to the inegalitarianism threatening the livelihoods of too many ordinary middle-class Americans. In this case, the ideological representations of any social reality are attempts to pervert, and then to placate, a basic instinct for equality – an instinct that may be kept down for a while but is constantly troubling, constantly trying to find its way back out into, the social formation that excludes it. This instinctual model is then used to support Ryan and Kellner's account of ideology – and, by association, of popular fantasy – as defence and it contributes to their strangely functionalist account of the relation between cinematic and social representation. There is (social) anxiety and then there is (cinematic) defence and films as disparate as *Jaws* (Spielberg 1975) and *The Exorcist* (Friedkin 1973) can be yoked together as evidence of 'anxieties generated by contemporary social movements like feminism and by the crisis in confidence in business and civic leadership' (ibid.: 57).

It is this type of collation which then informs Ryan and Kellner's interpretation of Coppola's films as forms of compensation for and defence against the current 'crises of the family, of the economy, and of public leadership' which are provoking 'increasingly aestheticist fantasies and regressive genre forms' (ibid.: 65–6). Coppola's films, the authors conclude, are 'authoritarian, petit bourgeois (small-business based), and neo-patriarchal', assuming increasingly 'overtly rightist forms' (ibid.: 66). Thus both *The Outsiders* and *Rumble Fish* can be understood as key examples of the reactionary and authoritarian fantasies of contemporary cinema: ' *The Outsiders* and *Rumble Fish* (both 1983) are about young boys yearning for strong leaders' and 'men either live separately from women in all-male groups or else violently reject women' (ibid.: 71–2). Paradoxically for this argument, however, the leader of the group satisfies a desire for the mother, for the omnipotent maternal presence of early infancy:

> The leader is someone who brooks no limitation on a triumph of his will; he represents a conservative male desire to regress to a narcissistic state in which all desires are immediately satisfied, especially by the mother. The perfect fusion of command and execution in the leadership principle is a correlate of the perfect

fusion of self and world, self and mother which the narcissistically wounded male child desires yet can never attain. The mother's ineluctable difference, experienced as a loss of object constancy, thus motivates the rightist political thematics.

(ibid.: 73)

There are links to be made between what Ryan and Kellner are saying here and the description of homo-erotic male bonding in *The Outsiders* as an ideal world which is 'both a womb and a locker room: no women need apply to this dreamy brotherhood' (Corliss 1983a: 78). If women are excluded from this fraternal tie, they are also, quite literally, its container; they are simultaneously inside and outside of the fantasmatic construction of brotherhood just as, for Ryan and Kellner, they are both violently rejected and over-whelmingly present. Further, and despite the fact that Ryan and Kellner situate their intervention as an attempt to construct a progressive politics of popular culture, the terms of their reading – narcissism, the perfect fusion of mother and child, a regressive desire for that fusion which lines up on the side of an illusory and extremist politics – reproduce the essential elements of a conservative and normative critique of a 'narcissistic crisis' in western culture. In particular, the equation of a fantasy of fusion with the mother with a desire for political authoritarianism depends on a rereading of the concept of narcissism which runs through recent responses to a (supposed) failure of authority and social identification – notably, Christopher Lasch's *The Culture of Narcissism* and Janine Chasseguet-Smirgel's *The Ego Ideal*, translated into English, with an introduction by Lasch, in 1985.

First published in 1979, Lasch's *The Culture of Narcissism: American Life in an Age of Diminishing Expectations* inserts itself as an 'explosive' and wideranging attempt to establish a link between the extension of capitalist economic individualism and social anomie, between 'narcissistic' preoccupation with self-gratification and a failure to internalize a strong social superego. 'The growth of bureaucracy', Lasch argues, 'creates an intricate network of personal relations, puts a premium on social skills, and makes the unbridled egotism of the American Adam untenable' (Lasch 1980: 11). The grandiose desires of the narcissistic personality type invest in illusory and idolized fantasies of self and other which erode established structures of authority and collectivity. Thus the culture of narcissism 'erodes all forms of patriarchal authority and . . . weakens the social superego, formerly represented by fathers, teachers, and preachers' (ibid.). In a response to Lasch in 1982, Michèle Barrett and Mary McIntosh drew attention to his 'unusual slot' as both a self-styled socialist with a high media profile and a best-selling author (Barrett and McIntosh 1982: 36). Given his sometimes virulent attack on feminism and his elegy for the patriarchal family, they also express concern at what was perceived as Lasch's growing influence on the 'left' in the United States and in Britain. That influence owes as much, if not more, I think, to the prevalence of an object-relations theory which focuses on the early mother–child bond as it does to any broad acceptance of Lasch's analysis: Lasch shares an emphasis on infantile fantasies of the maternal with otherwise disparate feminist critics (Chodorow 1978; Dinnerstein 1978; Benjamin 1978). His work also demonstrates how that emphasis, despite its influence on a feminist return to the pre-Oedipal mother–child dyad to try to theorize a beyond of the father and of Oedipal conflict for psychoanalysis, can so easily become a form of 'blaming the mother' for the social loss of paternal authority. On the one hand, that blaming is in a tradition of anxiety about the decline of American culture which runs through, randomly, Alvin Toffler's *Future Shock* (1970), William H. Whyte's *The Organization Man* (1956), Vance Packard's *The Hidden Persuaders* (1957), David Riesman's *The Lonely Crowd* (1950) and Betty Friedan's *The Feminine Mystique* (1963). To take just one example: both Toffler, in a section called 'The Fractured Family', and Lasch, in 'Paternalism Without Father', inflect anxiety through narratives of the loss of paternal authority – whether that authority is lost to mothers, to the mass media or to an ever more intrusive and omnipresent 'state'. Toffler's 'Communes and Homosexual Daddies', remarkable for its anticipation and inversion of Modleski's analysis of the loving paternity in 1980s cinema, insists, for example, on the media's participation in a 'softening up' of culture, on its role in 'preparing it for acceptance of the idea of child-rearing by men':

> [T]he mass media, in a strange non-conspiratorial fashion, appear to have decided simultaneously that men who raise children hold special interest for the public. Extremely popular television shows in recent seasons have glamourized womanless households in which men scrub floors, cook, and, most significantly, raise children. *My Three Sons, The Rifleman, Bonanza,* and *Bachelor Father* are four examples.
>
> (Toffler 1970: 227)

On the other hand, Lasch's concern about an assault on traditional forms of authority is indissociable from his psychoanalytic account of the changing face of pathology in contemporary America. 'The decline of institutionalised authority in an ostensibly permissive society', he suggests,

> does not, however, lead to a "decline of the superego" in individuals. It encourages instead the development of a harsh, punitive superego that derives most of its psychic energy, in the absence of authoritative social prohibitions, from the destructive, aggressive impulses within the id.
>
> (Lasch 1980: 11–12)

Lasch uses the example of the borderline patient to support his suggestion that a historical shift, taking place in the 1940s and 1950s, has produced a new type of client for psychiatry and psychoanalysis: the well-defined symptoms, the phobias, fixations and conversions of repressed sexual desire familiar to classical psychoanalysis have been displaced by 'diffuse dissatisfactions', feelings of purposelessness, depression and futility (ibid.: 37–8). That displacement, according to Lasch, has generated a 'new theory of narcissism' based on a distinction between a primary and a secondary or pathological form of narcissism which aims at the 'incorporation of grandiose object images as a defense against anxiety and guilt':

> Both types of narcissism blur the boundaries between the self and the world of objects, but there is an important difference between them. The newborn infant – the primary narcissist – does not yet perceive his mother as having an existence separate from his own, and he therefore mistakes dependence on the mother, who satisfies his needs as soon as they arise, with his own omnipotence . . . Secondary narcissism, on the other hand, 'attempts to annul the pain of disappointed [object] love' and to nullify the child's rage against those who do not respond immediately to his needs.
>
> (ibid.: 36)

Lasch gives such a range of sources for this description of a change in individual and social psycho-pathology that it is worth remembering the warning sounded by Laplanche and Pontalis – that primary narcissism has been subject to 'extreme variations in sense' (Laplanche and Pontalis 1973: 337). Very broadly, these variations are derived from a distinction, or the lack of a distinction, between auto-erotism and primary narcissism: if primary narcissism is understood as a primitive and objectless state of fusion with the mother which exists from the moment of the child's birth (if not before), then auto-erotism, as a stage prior to and supportive of the development of a capacity for narcissism disappears. In 'On Narcissism: An Introduction' (1914), Freud was clear that 'a unity comparable to the ego cannot exist in the individual from the start'; a 'new psychical action' has to be 'added' to the auto-erotic instincts, which are there from the start, 'in order to bring about narcissism' (*PFL* 11: 69). Lacan inflects this coincidence between primary narcissism and ego-formation as the ego's 'amorous captivation' with itself in the imaginary of the mirror stage (Laplanche and Pontalis 1973: 26; Lacan 1977). In this case, primary narcissism is the internalization of a relation which supports the identifications of the ego and continues to do so. It is not a stage which can be, in any simple sense, passed through. It is in fact our privilege, Lacan suggests, to see the 'veiled faces' of the imagos in 'our daily experience and in the penumbra of symbolic efficacity' (Lacan 1977: 3).

If, by contrast, primary narcissism is used to refer to a state of fusion and plenitude, secondary narcissism can be reduced to a more or less pathological regression or to an infantile yearning for what must inevitably be lost. On the one hand, the ego must have been there, in that state of fusion, in order to 'know' what it has lost – that is, the ego, however rudimentary, is always there. On the other hand, the ego has to learn to adapt to its loss of what it will remember as an ideal state, to overcome its desire for fusion in the name of independence and maturity. It is this second account of primary narcissism and the normative model of the ego derived from it that underlies Lasch's identification of a contemporary 'crisis of narcissism', a crisis generated by the failure to develop the kind of strong, boundaried ego which, as we've seen, has been so heavily invested by psychoanalytic and critical theories of collective identification. In 'The Freudian Left', Lasch refers to the form of regressive group identity with which Janine Chasseguet-Smirgel takes issue for its 'ideological' and 'perverse' attempt to evade development via a fantasy of fusion (Lasch, quoting Chasseguet-Smirgel, 1981: 32). Perversity, and ideology as perversity, is carrying the denial of the Oedipus complex and of the mother's castration for this account, a denial which both Lasch and Chasseguet-Smirgel equate with a desire for illusion, asylum and stasis. 'People no longer dream of overcoming difficulties', according to Lasch, 'but merely of surviving them . . . The normative concept of developmental stages promotes a view of life as an obstacle course: the aim is simply to get through the course with a minimum of trouble and pain' (Lasch 1980: 49). But if Lasch is distancing himself here from the sometimes insidious rhetoric of therapeutic sensibility and personal growth, it has also to be said that both he and Chasseguet-Smirgel invoke a no less normative passage through the Oedipus complex as the solution to a contemporary malaise. The failure to negotiate the Oedipus complex – to pass through the traumatic recognition of sexual difference and to identify 'properly' with the Oedipal law – locks narcissists, perverts and ideologists into their restless search for the object or group that will not disappoint them. Janine Chasseguet-Smirgel assimilates that search, and the political formations to which in her view it gives rise, to a desire for, and sometimes of, the 'mother of the pervert':

> An ideology always contains within it a phantasy of narcissistic assumption linked to a return to a state of primary fusion, which equally excludes conflict and castration and thus operates within the order of Illusion. The leader in these ideological groups does not appear to me to be a representation of the father. These groups aim at an eradication of the Oedipus complex and world of the father. The leader is an analogue of the mother of the pervert.
>
> (Chasseguet-Smirgel 1985: 193)

Thus a narcissistic desire for fusion with the mother is said to underlie both the desire for the types of authoritarian forms of political identification that Ryan and Kellner have in mind – Chasseguet-Smirgel detects a perverse illusion behind the most devastating myths of a *totale Staat* and the mass psychologies of the 1930s – *and* socially and politically marginalized group identifications. According to Lasch, for example, feminist separatism is no more than the 'dream of an island secure against male intrusion' (Lasch 1980: 199) or the symptom of a refusal to adapt to relations with men, to the demands of sexual difference: 'Raised to an ideology in recent movements for sexual separatism, this fantasy springs from a need not to recognize the mutual dependence of men and women' (Lasch 1985: xiii). In other words, it becomes possible to fault both mother and daughter for their collusion in a fantasy of a maternal presence which lacks nothing and seduces the daughter into a desire that, at the same time, sustains the mother in the narcissism of her position. The (perverse) mother of the pervert encourages the child's illusion that he or she can satisfy her: the pervert's claim is always 'I did not have to take my father's place, I always had it' (Chasseguet-Smirgel 1985: 12).

Lasch and Chasseguet-Smirgel are not alone in their contention that there is something other than a desire for post-Oedipal paternal authority, or authoritarianism, at stake in the fantasies supporting the forms of group identity and identification they are addressing. In 'Women's Time' – and famously – Julia Kristeva isolated the fantasy of an 'archaic, full, total englobing mother with no frustration, no separation' behind the political and social mobilizations which aim to counter the violence and the 'sacrifice' of the social contract (Kristeva 1986a: 205). 'Each time the mobilization takes place,' she insisted, whether 'in the name of a nation, of an oppressed group, of a human essence imagined as good and sound', it is actually occurring 'in the name . . . of a kind of fantasy of archaic fulfilment which an arbitrary, abstract and thus even bad and ultimately discriminatory order has come to disrupt' (ibid.: 204).

For a feminism that has, as Jacqueline Rose suggests, 'asked so much' of the mother–daughter relationship, Kristeva's critique is both difficult and essential – not least when it takes the form of a question: 'While that order is accused of being oppressive, is it not actually being reproached with being too weak, with not measuring up to this pure and good, but henceforth lost, substance' (Rose 1986: 160; Kristeva 1986a: 204). For Kristeva, this fantasy of archaic fulfilment has to be challenged if we are ever to move beyond an interminable oscillation between the authoritarianism of the Oedipal law and the pre-Oedipal love of an idealized maternal object. In this sense, her description of the process of abjection as the first attempt to separate from a 'clinging' or 'fused' mother, a 'false' mother who wraps herself around her child 'like a poultice', puts a brake on any such idealization by throwing the fused objectlessness of primary narcissism back onto auto-erotism, onto the impossible dyad in which 'the child and the mother do not yet constitute "two"' (Kristeva 1986b: 251; 256). But, and recalling Modleski's discontent with Kristeva's configuration of paternity, the imaginary father, the 'dazzling, domesticated paternity' which becomes the counterpart to an abject mother who has 'ceased to be a container of needs' risks reinstating the kind of sexual differentiation of the socializing process that, as we've seen, runs through Freud's theory (ibid.: 256; 260). Once again, a loving father constructs psychic and social space by acting as a 'magnet' for 'our idealizing constructions' while an archaic mother, 'magnet of desire and hatred, fascination and disgust', threatens to trap her child outside of the social-symbolic contract as a 'corpse under care' (ibid.: 374; 382). And, yet again, that child is more likely to be a daughter who all too easily 'connives' with her mother's difficulty in gaining access for herself or her children to the 'order of signs' (Kristeva 1986a: 204).

While in no sense simply reinvesting the fantasy of a totalizing good object in a paternal rather than a maternal substance, Kristeva's sexing of a social and loving identification lends itself to an otherwise paradoxical alliance with the calls for a reintegration of paternal authority coming from Lasch and Chasseguet-Smirgel. Paradoxical because Kristeva is explicit in her opposition to such calls: 'The crisis exists only for mirrors that are enamored of stable images'; 'There has been too much stress on the crisis in paternity as cause of psychotic discontent' (Kristeva 1987: 378). But whatever its resistance to any return to the 'fierce but artificial and incredible tyranny of the Law and the Superego' (ibid.), the figure of an archaic and loving father occludes the less social aspects of such a primal paternity; that is, it ignores the crucial shift in emphasis away from the perversity of the archaic mother to the pathology of the primal father, a shift that I attempted to trace earlier and that can be seen taking place, for example, through Adorno's critique. That shift complicates Kristeva's association between Freud's 'father of individual prehistory' and her concept of an imaginary father (Kristeva 1986b: 250; 1987) – a complication which, in turn, has decisive effects on the explanation of a desire for collective identification in terms of a regressive masculine (Ryan and Kellner) or narcissistic and perverse (Chasseguet-Smirgel and Lasch) wish for fusion with the mother.

The possibility of a pathological primal paternity undermines a tendency to lay claim to the father as a guarantor of reality against the dangers of fantasy or illusion, as guarantor of social cohesion against collective disintegration and aggression. The narcissism ascribed to the primal father in Freud's theory of group identity both disturbs the privileged link between narcissism and the maternal object and shows up a problem in the idealized form of social identification set against the culture of narcissism by Lasch and Chasseguet-Smirgel. However troubling their account of 'ideological' group identity is, it cannot be stressed too much that both the 'unbridled egotism' of the American Adam which Lasch compares favourably with the craving dependence of the contemporary narcissist and the 'world of the father' that Chasseguet-Smirgel fears is undermined by an eradication of the conflict of the Oedipus complex, rest on a category of narcissism. Compare, for example, Freud's sketch of the primal father as 'absolutely narcissistic, self-confident and independent' (*PFL* 12: 156) and the following passage from *The Culture of Narcissism*:

> For the narcissist, the world is a mirror, whereas the rugged individualist saw it as an empty wilderness to be shaped to his own design. In the nineteenth century American imagination, the . . . West represented an opportunity to build a new society un-encumbered by feudal inhibitions, but it also tempted man to throw off civilization and to revert to savagery. Through compulsive industry and relentless sexual repression, nineteenth-century Americans achieved a fragile triumph over the id. The violence they turned against the Indians and against nature orig-inated not in unrestrained impulse but in the white Anglo-Saxon superego, which feared the wildness of the West because it objectified the wildness within each individual. . . . In the heat of the struggle to win the West, the American pioneer gave full vent to his rapacity and murderous cruelty, but he always envisaged the result – not without misgivings, expressed in a nostalgic cult of lost innocence – as a peaceful, respectable, churchgoing com-munity safe for his women and children. He imagined that his offspring, raised under the morally refining influence of feminine 'culture,' would grow up to be sober, law-abiding, domesticated American citizens, and the thought of the advantages they would inherit justified his toil and excused, he thought, his frequent lapses into brutality, sadism and rape.
>
> (Lasch 1980: 10–11)

As the very foundation of the American *polis*, the rugged indi-vidualist and his white Anglo-Saxon superego represents the cele-brated counter-image of the narcissist. Lasch maps the distinctions between real development and regressive self-interest, between Oedipal adaptation and narcissistic infantilism, on to a historical difference between the nineteenth and twentieth centuries. Standing against the 'annihilating boredom' of contemporary American cul-ture and the 'new executive, boyish, playful and "seductive"' (ibid.: 44), the American Adam is the compound figure behind a myth of social origin. Rapist and husband, murderer and father, savage and model citizen, his unbridled egotism founds a social order prepared to find consolation for his 'lapses' in the domestic and civic fantasies that simultaneously support them.

At the same time, this egotism implicates Lasch's critique in the promotion of a type of independence which bears an almost uncanny resemblance to the narcissism of Freud's primal father. The dissociality of that narcissism appears throughout 'Group Psychology and the Analysis of the Ego' (1921) in which Narcissus is used to explain not only the origin of social identification but social identification as such. In 1921, Freud insists on the relation to the primal father as the model for a very contemporary form of group identification:

> The members of the group were subject to ties just as we see them today, but the father of the primal horde was free. His intellectual acts were strong and independent even in isolation, and his will needed no reinforcement from others. Consistency leads us to assume that his ego had few libidinal ties; he loved no one but himself, or other people only in so far as they served his needs . . . Even to-day the members of a group stand in need of the illusion that they are equally and justly loved by their leader; but the leader himself need love no one else, he may be of a masterful nature, absolutely narcissistic, self-confident and independent.
>
> (*PFL* 12: 155–56)

Thus 'even today', even in 1921, when the fascist ideologues were exploiting the same nineteenth-century crowd psychologists on whose work Freud was drawing for his analyses of mass identity and identification, the 'leader of the group is still the dreaded primal father' (ibid.: 160). The elements of mass psychology isolated by, amongst others, Le Bon and Tarde, and for which Freud wants to account – imitative suggestibility, coercive fascination, the demand to be loved by the leader – are derived in Freud's model from an 'aptitude for reviving old situations', from a 'predisposition which has survived in the unconscious from the early history of the human family' (ibid.). In one sense, like the 'purest and truest' type of woman to whom we saw Freud succumbing in his investigations into feminine narcissism, the leader occupies the limit point of the narcissistic libidinal position. Unlike the woman, he neither loves nor demands love from the other. In 1914, Freud was clear (if not coherent once we take the dependence of a specifically feminine narcissism into account) that while narcissism may be 'unassailable' – the narcissist loves no one so much as himself – it is also pathological. Loving himself, the narcissist does not need to be loved and so does not suffer the anxiety that the fear of losing love subjects us to. But he also falls ill: 'A strong egoism is a protection against falling ill, but in the last resort we must begin to love in order not to fall ill, and we are bound to fall ill if, in consequence of frustration, we are unable to love' (*PFL* 11: 78). The masculine omnipotence of the primal Narcissus fails, then, in the face of Freud's insistence on both the pathology and the femininity of the narcissistic position. That failure unsettles the social effectivity ascribed to Narcissus who receives a demand for love from the group that, at the same time, loves him for his narcissistic refusal to love. '[H]e loved no one but himself' but the members of the group 'stand in need of the illusion that they are equally and justly loved by their leader'. Clearly, the group tie to the leader cannot be one of harmonious complementarity between a loving Narcissus and his desiring subjects because Narcissus does not love – a discrepancy which suggests a question about how and why this structure works, or how Freud's theory makes it work. On the one hand, Freud is restating the essential role of fantasy in the social process. It is the *illusion* of the father/leader's love desired by the group, an illusion which reinflects the demand for love as a demand for the fiction or the fantasy of paternal love. In other words, there is a shift from a demand for the libidinal tie to the object towards a desire for a libidinized fiction – the fiction of a loving paternity or an idealizing fantasy of the loving father. On the other hand, Freud invests the group with an insatiable desire for authority which does not balk at the fundamental masochism written into the libidinal tie to Narcissus. Loving authority presents itself here in its very refusal to satisfy the demand for love; it imposes privation as proof of the love it withholds.

If, as I suggested in the previous chapter, we can read Freud's myth of Narcissus as a fantasy of origins, then the repetition between Lasch and Freud may be symptomatic insofar as it allows the figure of the primal father to present himself as an insistent object of social fantasy – as the representative of all fathers, of all leaders, once and for all: 'The leader of the group is still the dreaded primal father; the group still wishes to be governed by unrestricted force; it has an extreme passion for authority; in Le Bon's phrase, it has a thirst for obedience' (*PFL* 12: 160). Narcissus is there too in Ryan and Kellner's leader who 'brooks no limitation on a triumph of his will', who represents the 'perfect fusion of command and execution' that young boys will yearn for (Ryan and Kellner 1990: 73). The repetition of Narcissus across these readings is not in itself surprising given Freud's direct or indirect influence on their authors but its very influence suggests the virtually paradigmatic status of the fantasy which is structuring Freud's own analysis. Borch-Jacobsen, for example, has concluded that Freud does not so much 'analyze this totalitarian fantasy as subscribe to it' (Borch-Jacobsen 1991: 69). Similarly, Philippe Lacoue-Labarthe and Jean-Luc Nancy have argued that

> Freud seems never to have really shaken off this Narcissus. Even when he recognizes it as a theoretical fiction, he emphasizes all the more its function: the Narcissus is the ultimate object of the *theory*, it offers the theory its ultimate figure as a *visible form*, and so assures the identity of psychoanalysis.
>
> (Lacoue-Labarthe and Nancy 1989: 201)

What these readings suggest, in turn, is that only by putting the figure of Narcissus back into the various models of group identification we've been examining, can we start to interpret the visibility, the specularity of masculinity and the fantasies of collective identification in Coppola's *Rumble Fish*. To anticipate: the social, fictional and theoretical effectiveness of (Freud's?) Narcissus can be used to start to clarify the collective identifications at work in and through this film insofar as those identifications depend on *making* the myth of a simultaneously loving and omnipotent Narcissus work – the myth which is essential both to the representation of the group tie in the film narrative and to the identifications passing between the spectator and the screen.

We have already started to trace these identifications through the different critical responses to *Rumble Fish*. The politics of the group identification invested by the film have been read in at least two different ways. For Ryan and Kellner, clearly, *Rumble Fish* is endorsing a misogynistic and conservative, if not totalitarian, version of the social bond. By contrast, Mark Spratt, in 'Rebels, Rumbles and Motorcycle Boys', published in *Cinema Papers* in 1984, places *Rumble Fish* as a film which inherits the 'born to be wild' ethos bequeathed by the cinema of the 1950s and 1960s. That ethos, he suggests, has been squandered by a cinematic representation of an adolescent subculture which has lost the dream: 'Motorbikes seem to have become transport, not proud stallions carrying wild boys and girls towards their dreams' (Spratt 1984: 309). In this case, the failure to imagine the motorcycle beyond its use value is made symptomatic of the facile materialism that Spratt detects in 1980s cinema. This account of the malaise afflicting contemporary film lines up, I think, as a countercultural version of Lasch's lament for an Anglo-Saxon superego – a malaise that *Rumble Fish* together with *Fast Talking* (Cameron 1984) and *Reckless* (Foley 1984) is seen to resist or work against. All three films feature a 'male teenage hero living in similar stressful home and social situations . . . [and] looking for a way out' symbolized by the motorcycle (ibid.: 310). Spratt gives the following plot summary of *Rumble Fish*:

> Rusty-James (Matt Dillon) is a 14-year-old living with his alcoholic father (Dennis Hopper) in Tulsa, Oklahoma. His mother deserted the family when he was two years old. Rusty-James idolizes his elder brother, known as the Motorcycle Boy (Mickey Rourke), who has a reputation as a gang leader. Rusty-James tries to emulate this tough leadership but gets expelled from school and loses his girlfriend Patty (Diane Lane). The Motorcycle Boy has made a bike trip to California and back, and becomes fascinated by the Siamese 'rumble fish' in the pet shop. He is killed in his attempt to liberate the fish and Rusty-James takes his motor-cycle to ride off to fulfil the Motorcycle Boy's ambitions and find his own.
>
> (ibid.: 310)

Spratt's generic stabilization of the film here rests on his decision to read the relation between the brothers as one that mimes both the identification between a model-leader and a subject who desires to be like him and the classic fraternal alliance between (oppositional, rebellious) brothers. Crudely, Spratt suspends *Rumble Fish* somewhere between the group fantasy of Narcissus and the bond of brotherhood. At the same time, that suspension occludes what is most difficult about the film – the ambivalence which is introduced into the relation between the brothers by the Motorcycle Boy's death. Crucially, something is lost when the Motorcycle Boy's fascination with the rumble fish is understood simply as a desire to free them (a desire which can then be said to transgress a jealous and persecutory law) and, further, when what passes between Rusty-James and his brother is regarded as a form of idealized inheritance. To put this another way: Spratt insists on a type of inheritance without trauma which both silences the aggression internal to the younger brother's desire *to be like* (again, recall Borch-Jacobsen: 'I want what my brother, my model, my idol wants: and I want it in his place') and passes over the question of precisely what it means to be possessed by the dead in this way; that is, the question of how the ambitions of a dead man can even start to be fulfilled?[7] These questions are made all the more urgent by the film's ambiguous insistence on the Motorcycle Boy's death as something other than the result of a murderous persecution by the law – the persecution which would produce the category of the ideal rebel. That ideal, and with it the transmission and identification between the brothers, is fatally complicated by a sense that the Motorcycle Boy's death is not a murder but a suicide – the brother's own desire for death which then sets up another coincidence between aggressive masculinity and the rumble fish who 'kill themselves fighting their own reflection' and, decisively, what seems to be an unexpected and unsettling identification between the Motorcycle Boy and the law.

A problematic coincidence with the law could be said to govern the ambivalent, frequently bewildering, relation between the Motorcycle Boy and the police officer, Patterson. In his review of *Rumble Fish* for *Sight and Sound*, Chris Auty comments on how he came up against something inhabiting the film and blocking his attempts to tell its 'story', to say what it is 'really' about. Like Spratt, Auty reads the death of the Motorcycle Boy as 'inevitable', as an act of liberation (Auty 1984: 152). Unlike Spratt, he finds the substance of the film elsewhere, in the enigma that he links to whatever is taking place between the Motorcycle Boy and Patterson:

> The Bike Boy is truly a figure briefly returned from the dead – an unexpected, unwelcome visitor eventually killed for keeps by the bullet of the town's unforgiving cop. What it is from the past that needs to be forgiven never becomes entirely clear.
>
> (ibid.)

In turn, that obscurity depends on a secret apparently known to both the Motorcycle Boy and to Patterson but not to Rusty-James whose bewilderment mirrors, or carries, the spectator's own confusion through a set of exchanges which confirm something like an identification of desire between the law and its seeming opponent. Tentatively, one key scene between Patterson and the two brothers establishes a contract, or a promise, between the Motorcycle Boy and the police officer. Increasingly anxious about his brother's sanity, Rusty-James follows the Motorcycle Boy to the pet store where Patterson confronts them both. The police officer's threat to the Motorcycle Boy – 'Somebody ought to get you off the streets' – prompts a response which is both a challenge and an appeal –

'Somebody ought to put the fish back in the river'. On the one hand, that challenge sets up a more or less conventional parallel between the rebel 'looking for a way out' and the rumble fish who might stop fighting themselves if they were put back into the river – if they had, in the Motorcycle Boy's words, 'the room to live'. On the other hand, the possibility that the Motorcycle Boy is letting the police officer know that he intends to raid the pet store is confirmed by a brief image of Patterson, waiting outside the store before any official alert has been given, waiting to shoot the Motorcycle Boy as he emerges with the rumble fish.

The unstable legacy of the Motorcycle Boy, then, is the desire for his own death which mimics the law's opposition to him, or, more specifically, to his return. Thus the identification between the brothers is fatally twisted because that desire turns Rusty-James's wish to be like his brother into a wish for identification at its most violent edge – into identification with an ideal that wants to die. In this sense, the film is reinflecting the aggression internal to that wish to be in the brother's place as the ideal's own desire for death. One effect of that reinflection is to make the identifying younger brother innocent of aggression. The other is to invest the figure of an idealized leader who not only resists Spratt's generic celebration of the 'wild boy' myth but also skews Ryan and Kellner's account of the strong leader that they find represented through, or more cynically, promoted by, *Rumble Fish*. In fact, the attachment to the myth of Narcissus *within* this critique could be said to make itself felt when Ryan and Kellner describe the Motorcycle Boy as a 'visionary, natural leader':

> Like the colored fish (which only the visionary, natural leader, The Motorcycle Boy, has the power to see), ordinary things are endowed with transcendental, highly metaphoric significance through the use of nonrealist camera angles, speeded-up film, and fantasy sequences, strategies that evoke an attitude of veneration parallel to that inspired by leaders, a sense of the mysterious, transcendental power or meaning in things. If the all-male group is a defense against women so also is the representational form of the film.
>
> (Ryan and Kellner 1990: 73–4)

In this remarkable passage the film itself, in particular its implicitly 'masculinist' aesthetics, is equated with the kind of leader that Ryan and Kellner repudiate. (Once again, this is cinema, or the culture industry, as a type of perverse or regressive father-leader.) But the authors symptomatically invert the relation between the Motorcycle Boy's look and the aesthetic surface of the film when they single him out as the one who can see the colours of the fish, and by association who can decode the metaphor, or the bewilderment, of the film. In fact, the film is explicit: the Motorcycle Boy cannot see colours. Colour-blind and half-deaf from the gang fights he used to lead, the Motorcycle Boy's perception of the world is, as he says, like 'black and white tv with the sound turned low' – a description which can easily be applied to the entire film. What the Motorcycle Boy sees and hears, then, is what the spectator (with the one *exception* of the coloured fish) sees and hears, a mapping which refuses the singularity ascribed to the film's 'Narcissus' by Ryan and Kellner. At the same time, the coincidence between the spectator and Narcissus carries its own form of disturbance since the aural and visual identification between the Motorcycle Boy and the spectators suggests a necessary identification, or a collusion, with him as one of the conditions of watching the film as such. That identification is then necessarily caught up in the fatality which, I think, the film introduces into the category of narcissism. It is difficult to reconcile the 'perfect fusion of command and execution' that Ryan and Kellner detect in the Motorcycle Boy with his malaise – a malaise which may have nothing to do with an adequation between desire and execution: 'He was born in the wrong era, on the wrong side of the river, with the ability to do anything he wants to do, and finding nothing that he wants to do.' Compare this – his father's description of him to Rusty-James – with the Motorcycle Boy's own statement of his failure: 'I'm sorry I'm not the kind of brother you want but I can't be what I want to be any more than you can.' Thus both the dismissal and the celebration of *Rumble Fish* as a fantasy of either (or both) conservative or oppositional group identification answers 'no' to an idealizing question about the Motorcycle Boy which runs through the film – 'Is there anything he can't do?' – and immediately closes down the film's examination of the pathology of that omnipotence. Reinforcing Auty's sense that the Motorcycle Boy is in fact dead before the film begins, that pathology starts to show up as what Lacan, following Ernest Jones, describes as *aphanisis*, the death of desire itself. The 'absolute independence' of Freud's Narcissus and the egotism of the leader who brooks no limitation to his will – the narcissism, in short, required to sustain the fiction of a loving omnipotence – is confounded by the loss of a desire which can, in fact, only be missing because to be (found) wanting would immediately fracture narcissistic self-sufficiency.

This seems to be close to Lasch's critique of narcissism as precisely anomie or malaise. But the malaise afflicts the very figure of mythical independence through which Lasch aims to reconstruct the socio-political sphere. Put this way, the Motorcycle Boy becomes the embodiment of what Spratt presents as the failure of contemporary cinema to symbolize desire, a failure which then issues in the conformity with which he and Lasch are, though differently, so uncomfortable. This link between rebellion and conformity reinforces the uncertainty introduced by *Rumble Fish* into the opposition between a conservative authoritarianism and its progressive opponent. But the uncertainty goes further than this. The crucial dislocation between Rusty-James's desire to be like and the Motorcycle Boy's refusal even to be recalls Freud's analysis of the group tie constituted through the demand for love made on a Narcissus loved precisely because he does not love. We are then left with the question that haunts Freud's work: how and why does this mythic structure work? How and why does *Rumble Fish* work as a stunning instance of cinema's idealization of masculinity and of Narcissus? Reading across from Freud's 'Group Psychology and the Analysis of the Ego' to Coppola's *Rumble Fish* we might say that, both inside and outside of the film narrative, there is a demand for love structuring the ties to the Motorcycle Boy – a demand that makes more intelligible the masochism, or, more strongly, the death drive, apparently written into the spectatorial position. Certainly, the film's display of masculine beauty has to be put in the context not only of its 'unconscious' homo-eroticism but of this loving identification or demand. Remember, though, that it is the *fiction* of Narcissus's love that his subjects want – the fiction which releases them into an alliance with one another *against him*. In *Rumble Fish*, that fiction is staged through the death of the Motorcycle Boy and Rusty-James's ambiguous appropriation of his brother's role. But, as we've seen, the spectator is also required to identify with the Motorcycle Boy, to take on his look and, with it, his death. Not until the final frames of the film, after the Motorcycle Boy's death, do we see, albeit briefly, 'in colour'. Thus it is as though *Rumble Fish*, and its spectators, are suspended between the surface of the film made over to the Motorcycle Boy and its fiction which falls, more or less easily, into a narrative of fraternal rebellion and release.

From this point of speculation about what could be described as the spectator's suicidal identification with the film, we can also bring back the question, left in suspense since the beginning of this chapter, regarding the function and fantasy of the feminine in Coppola's cinema. In the first place, the exclusion and stereotyping of the woman through *Rumble Fish* is almost too insistent: the girlfriend whom Rusty-James imagines revealing herself to him dressed in black lingerie; the 'hooker on strip' (S.E. Hinton); the absent mother whose eccentricity or insanity the Motorcycle Boy is said to take on and who lives in California with 'a fucking movie producer' – a mother who is thereby equated with the dream factory itself; the beautiful wild girl high on heroin (another image of California) who 'doesn't know she's dying even when you show her the marks'; and, finally, Cassandra, the junkie whose knowledge of the Motorcycle Boy's return is given an ambiguous and prophetic status: 'I thought he'd gone for good. And I was wrong. But I was right.' Second, the stereotyping of the woman appears to mediate the fantasy of masculinity as both narcissistic and collective. That mediation shows most clearly through the Motorcycle Boy's former lover, Cassandra, who becomes a target for Rusty-James's aggression – aggression which can be read quite straightforwardly either as a symptom of sibling rivalry or of homo-eroticized fraternal desire. But the younger brother's antagonistic encounters with Cassandra also suggest another coincidence between the brothers and the law. In this case, the apparently unmotivated, excessive – and therefore bewildering – violence which characterizes Rusty-James's response to Cassandra mirrors Patterson's unexplained antagonism towards the Motorcycle Boy. The film draws attention to that mirroring through the question Cassandra puts to Rusty-James: 'Why do you dislike me so much? I've always tried to be your friend.' It is a question which repeats, and so returns to him, the younger brother's uncomprehending interrogation of Patterson's hatred for the Motor-cycle Boy: 'Why do you hate him so much?' In this sense, as she becomes the privileged object of the younger brother's hatred, the idealizing aggression which is written out of, or occluded within, Rusty-James's wish to identify with, to be like his brother, is transferred onto the woman. In this sense, again, the woman is called upon to negotiate the ambivalence of the identifications supposed to constitute both the love for Narcissus and the group tie; she is the object through which the violence inseparable from idealization can take place.

As such, and as we saw in relation to Freud's myth of social origins, the woman can have no place in that fraternal bond. This is a femininity bereft of social fantasy (though no less fantasmatic for that), a femininity required to bereave itself in and through its mediation of the brothers' desire and its identification with the absent desire of Narcissus. There are, remember, no vicissitudes, no fantasmatic 'as if', for the woman/daughter who supports the perverse omnipotence of Narcissus – who becomes the object so empty that even Narcissus can want her without exposing any lack. That emptiness and its bereavement starts to suggest why the image of the woman is so insistently clichéd through the film and, perhaps, why the image of S.E. Hinton discussed at the beginning of this chapter seems to *shadow* Coppola's *Rumble Fish*. Both the image and the writing of S.E. Hinton – the image of her and the cinematic images generated by her work – demonstrate the overwhelming difficulty of making the difference, of what it would take to put the woman back differently into a bond – fraternal, narcissistic and fantasmatic – which thrives on a form of seduction which can turn even death into a pleasure. At the same time, and finally, the transference of violence and bereavement onto the woman says something about why the film can risk the ambivalence of its Narcissus without failing in its idealization of masculinity. That transference bears witness to an identification which can be called upon to support the omnipotent pathology of Narcissus – even in the face of his inertia – and can be found so often in the critical responses to the Motorcycle Boy as an ideal figure, as 'an idol . . . an enigma – as charming to the audience out here as he is to the audience of hangers-on that he would vaguely like to cast off in the film' (Auty 1984: 152). Like the woman, cast in the role of hanger-on, this spectator is essential to the film's fantasy-structure of a narcissistic and fraternal alliance which has never been, which can only come into being with the collusion of the spectators – male or female – who look at the screen and see in the Motorcycle Boy 'a young god with a mortal wound' (Kroll 1983: 128).

Chapter 5

Lost Angels

River's Edge and social spectatorship

The chief charges were 1) that she was dead, and therefore could not hold any property whatsoever; 2) that she was a woman, which amounts to much the same thing.

(Virginia Woolf, *Orlando: A Biography*)

What happens if a real event that generates anxiety about looking as a threat to the social bond is turned into cinema? The following reports from *The Los Angeles Times* and *The New York Times* in November and December 1981 give the first accounts of a murder that took place in Milpitas, California in that year:

More than a dozen high school students who viewed the strangled body of a schoolmate kept her murder a secret to protect the youth who bragged of killing her and proudly showed off the corpse, officials said Tuesday. [Detective] Icely, who interviewed thirteen students who had gone to the murder site, said that the youths were callous and cold, with no apparent feelings for Miss Conrad. 'Their prime objective was to cover up for their friend. They showed no remorse at all for the girl lying in the ravine . . . I just couldn't believe it. Most people who see a homicide are happy to talk about it . . . ' Mike Irvin, 18, an auto assembly worker, was the first to notify police of the murder. He heard from friends at Milpitas High that a corpse was in the hills. 'All the kids wanted to go up and see her,' he said. 'As soon as I saw it was a body and not a mannequin, I went straight to the police.'

(*The Los Angeles Times*, 25 November 1981)

To Detective Sgt. Gary Meeker of the Santa Clara Sheriff's Department, it was not the killing of 14-year-old Marcy Renee Conrad that was so unusual, at least not these days. 'Not the crime,' said the 42-year-old sergeant, who has been a police officer all his working life, like his father before him. 'The unusual aspect was what followed, the kids going up there. That was the unusual aspect.' At that, he said, it was only the extremity of the crime, the strangulation of a young girl, that made the callousness and silence of the teen-agers so out of the ordinary. For two days they had gone up into the hills by the carload, as if on an outing, to take a look at the body lying half naked in the woods.

(*The New York Times*, 14 December 1981)

The killing of a high school student, Marcy Conrad, by fellow student, Anthony Broussard, received wide media coverage in the United States as an instance of outrageous social disaffection. Reports followed that the young woman's body had been stoned and covered with leaves (*The New York Times*, 25 November 1981). One of the students was quoted as saying, '"I didn't think it was real. I didn't think anything about it. I went home and partied"' (*The Los Angeles Times*, 2 December 1981) and police officers involved with the case repeatedly described the 'callousness' and indifference which seemed to mark the students' response – or lack of response – to what they had seen. One explanation after another was invoked by local authority figures and by the media to try to account for what had happened. The stepfather of one of the teenagers who did report the murder suggested that '"maybe its [sic] just that these are the kids of the people who were part of the '60s. Are they an offspring of the 'let's do your own thing' generation? I think we have to ask what has happened to our society, not just to our kids"' (*The Los Angeles Times*, 2 December 1981). The same report from *The Los Angeles Times* draws attention to the loyalty felt towards Broussard by those who considered themselves his friends, a loyalty which emerges as essentially gendered: '"It's hard to tell on somebody who's been your friend for 10 years," said Mark Fowlkes, 17, who considered himself the best friend of the student charged with murder. Fowlkes also was a former boyfriend of the victim.'

Working betwen the real event, a social trauma and the cinematic institution, *River's Edge* was released five years later in 1986. Directed by Tim Hunter from a screenplay by Neal Jiminez, the film was immediately taken up as a reconstruction or, worse, as a potentially unlimited replay, of the murder and of what took place afterwards. A successful campaign led by the Mayor of Milpitas,

Robert Livengood, and its 'city fathers', banned the film from being shown in the town. Livengood claimed that there was

'a feeling in Milpitas we didn't want our noses rubbed in this again . . . Everybody in this community has been beaten up – it's over for us. We've been through the process of mourning, we've had our catharsis and we don't need to go through it again.'

(Abramson 1987: 25)

Similarly, Milpitas Citizen of the Year, housewife Fifi Bradley, insisted that the film should have been called 'Sewer's Edge', that it was a 'sick' film about a 'sick' thing (ibid.). These reactions recall the controversies about 'image ethics' which have always accompanied documentary film-making insofar as documentary aims, at some level, to represent what is real. But although *River's Edge* inevitably situates itself within these debates, it should also be said that it does not attempt to recreate a factual account of the Milpitas killing. Neal Jiminez explicitly distanced his screenplay from Milpitas, stressing that he was drawing on his experience of a more general youth malaise:

'I'm writing about people I knew. There was the same kind of aimlessness to the kids I went to school with [in Sacramento]. It was a time when there wasn't a lot for kids to care about and not a lot of examples to follow.'

(ibid.)

At the same time, the film does not seem to have been criticized for a failure to tell the truth. Objections are couched in vaguer terms – *River's Edge* is depressing, sick, it won't let the town forget its 'shame'.

The police officer's shock at what he describes as the lack of remorse shown for the dead girl, when he is commenting not on Broussard but on the students who went to look at the body, suggests one way into what might be taking place in the reactions to *River's Edge*. Above all, perhaps, it was the students' 'silence' – their failure to say the right thing to the right people at the right time – which fuelled anxiety about what had 'gone wrong' with the kids in Milpitas and, by extension, with 'kids today'. Further, in its association with a communal act of looking at a dead body, that silence threatened to transform the students' 'unusual' lack of interest into a more pervasive form of social disintegration: '"I think we have to ask what has happened to our society, not just to our kids."' That

is, the teenagers were condemned for what they did not do when they
failed to publicize a murder, when they were not 'happy' to talk
about what must never remain a private event. Their public silence
ensured that their looking was felt to be affectless and asocial as, by
apparently failing to mourn the loss of a friend (or at least one of
their crowd), the students became 'spectators' but not 'witnesses'.
That is, 'what happened' in Milpitas brings us up against the social
dimension of spectatorship at its point of failure – a failure which
then threatens both to universalize the murderous aggression of the
event and to disperse a loss of affect across the social. It is as if a
loss of feeling associated both with youth and with an act of looking
has turned Wilhelm Reich's famous question around: we are left
asking not where misery comes from but where misery has gone.[1] In
other words, what happened set up a demand for a way of talking
about the effects of what doesn't happen, about a type of symbolic
omission and about a kind of dereliction of self in the role of
spectator. Not narrative truth, then, but something about the disturbing coincidence between whatever was being courted in those
expeditions out in the hills and the kind of looking beyond the pale
which takes place in cinema is at stake when Milpitas – and then
River's Edge – come to stand for a social made derelict through
dissociated looking.

LOOKING BEYOND THE PALE

A 'postmodern' and mediatized form of voyeurism is, perhaps, most
frequently called upon to 'explain' Milpitas – not only in the
constant references, at the time of the killing, to the loss of reality
and feeling caused by over-exposure to cinema and television but
also in an appropriation of one particular version of the 'Milpitas
killing' which was taken up as part of the reception of ('brat pack'
author) Bret Easton Ellis's first novel, *Less Than Zero*. In a review
of *Less Than Zero* which coincided with its first British publication
in 1986, Michael Pye drew on an apocryphal account of what
happened in Milpitas to support the truth value of Ellis's fiction, of
a 'new breed of young people' that has 'dispensed with feelings':

> Now Melrose Avenue is a strip of chic and posers, the best
> equivalent in all LA of a King's Road . . . You go there for a view
> of a new sort of kid that just visits the world, doesn't live here –
> that at 20 has had all the sex, drugs, rock 'n' roll and anomie the

human frame can stand. Their blank eyes, behind the two-tone Ray-Bans, are the horror in Bret Easton Ellis's first novel *Less Than Zero*, written when he was 20. The best-selling Melrose bible doesn't have murder, but it does have people watching – watching snuff films, watching a 12-year-old tied up and gang-raped, watching a mate make commercial love with an out-of-town businessman to support his drug habit. Everyone watches, everything might be for sale, everyone lives in the same solipsistic world where movie deals are the best connection the kids can imagine.

(Pye 1986: 49)

The terrain is familiar: twenty years on from the generation that made a difference, the 1980s becomes the decade of the so-called 'no power generation', famous, as we've seen, for a facile and materialistic conformity, or, crudely, for shopping rather than politics:

Ellis says his generation screws around, but they wait to ask about diseases when they're half undressed. They do drugs, but privately . . . The paisley shirts and psychedelic rock aren't so much a true Sixties' revival as another pointer to a failure of originality, not knowing what to want.

(ibid.)

While it remains unclear what a 'true' sixties revival might be or what exactly is lost when the 'new sort of kid' worries about sexually transmissible diseases, it is obvious that Pye is binding a supposed failure of the political and cultural imagination to looking as such:

Ellis's book is an outsider's view – chilly, ferocious and brilliantly done, but still someone who only watches . . . So the lovely, blank-eyed kids do just what they want, and anything's possible, even the worst. That is why the kids on Melrose fascinate. They're so blank they are ground for our fantasies, for the fantasy in *Less Than Zero*, as well as their own. Only the old people try not to look, and that's because they live there.

(ibid.)

The logic of this reference to the 'old people', living in the 'Golden Age' retirement home close to Melrose Avenue, constructs looking as a death threat to living. It's not only that if you live in the real world you have to do more than look but that there are some things you should not be able to bear to look at. In other words, if we are going to maintain the distinction between being dead and being alive, something about looking has to remain intolerable – something that, Pye insists, has been lost. Further, and crucially, if we think 'the picture sounds exaggerated then here's a case which might change your mind':

> It happened four years ago, one autumn day. A kid of 17 went driving in the hills with his girlfriend of 14. He stripped her, raped and killed her and brought his friends to see the corpse. They thought it was cool, even organized expeditions to see the body in the hills. One boy covered her with leaves 'because she was naked and I felt it was the right thing to do'. But nobody said anything, because the body was just a peepshow. At the kid's trial, lawyers said he was 'without emotion, as if nothing touched him', a schizophrenic with brain damage from chronic drug abuse, 'without feeling about human life'. He was sent away for life, and that left the other boys' parents to worry about their kids. Of course, they couldn't be doing such things – but how would the parents ever know? That's the possibility in the blank Melrose faces: that you might go to see your buddy's buddy's corpse, and, hell, a killer ain't nothing but a supplier. And that is the warning Ellis means to sound – to parents, especially.
>
> (ibid.)

Pye's retelling demonstrates how 'Milpitas' starts to circulate and to fuel what Leonard Grossberg, also commenting on Bret Easton Ellis, has described as a 'vague discomfort – if not outright paranoia – about the new generation of youth' (Grossberg 1988: 125). There is a decision here to explain the looking in Ellis's novel in terms of the looking in Milpitas and then to assimilate both to a pervasive form of disaffected voyeurism – a decision which makes itself felt, for example, in the eroticization implicit in 'stripped her, raped and killed her' and in the idea of the body as a 'peepshow', as a tantalizing and erotic image. One of the effects of this decision, in turn, is that voyeurism, or a perversion of looking, is allowed to persist as a sole category of explanation even when, especially when, it cannot quite account for the difference of whatever was taking place. The 'spectators' in Milpitas did not look illegitimately or intrusively at a private event which they then threatened to expose. Instead they turned around the public–private opposition of a classical voyeurism by looking at a murdered body – a body which always demands public exposure – and then refusing the cheerful discourse of homicide: 'Most people who see a homicide', according to the police officer who interviewed the students, 'are happy to talk about it' (*The Los Angeles Times*, 25 November 1981). At the same time, the eyewitness statement cited by Pye – 'One boy covered her with leaves "because she was naked and I thought it was the right thing to do"' – complicates the voyeuristic and sexually sadistic homogeneity being ascribed to the onlookers. An idea of the 'right thing to do' filters through here as an act of covering up, an act defined by a precarious ethical sense which implicates that 'right thing' itself in a sexualized look at the dead woman – the 'right thing' refers as much to her nakedness as to her death.

But if this is not, or not simply, voyeurism, then what is it? – and what is its shock if not that of a murderously perverse desire to look? We can start to question the difference of what doesn't happen in the spectatorship identified by the responses to Milpitas through two novels by Bret Easton Ellis, *Less Than Zero* (1985) and, more briefly, *American Psycho* (1991). Both novels, *American Psycho* in particular, have been received as exemplary instances of a new type of individual and collective desolation, of an anomic and alienated culture of nihilism. A month before its first British publication, Christopher Hudson reviewed *American Psycho* for the *Evening Standard* and described the book as both repugnant and dangerous. 'I am reviewing it early', he explained, 'in the hope that libraries won't order it, booksellers won't stock it and newspaper editors won't feel obliged to send hacketts to interview its smooth-talking author' (Hudson 1991: 36). Hudson condemns the novel first on obvious grounds – the clinical descriptions of sado-masochistic murder which presumably informed the decision made by its first American publishers, Simon and Schuster, to drop the novel on grounds of taste. But he also takes the new publishers, Picador, to task for 'deliberately aiming it at the mass market': 'Bret Easton Ellis, Brat Pack author of the bestselling *Less Than Zero*, has a powerful enough imagination to draw lesser, sicker minds into emulating his sex-crime fantasies' (ibid.).

In other words, when it is made 'freely' available in the high street, *American Psycho* breaches the boundaries which should have been set by the element of hard-core porn that made the book so notorious. As a mass cultural form, *American Psycho* becomes available to those 'lesser, sicker minds' – and what kind of disrespect is this? – which, left alone, would never have been able to imagine the things that happen in this book or even, it seems, have made their way to the kind of shops specializing in, and to some extent containing, the fantasies it is so haphazardly selling. At the same time, and Hudson insists on this, the novel refuses the anguish that just might have contained it – outside the porn shop – within a literary aesthetic defined by its commitment:

> If there had been some anguished purpose behind these obscenities – for instance, to reflect upon man or his society in extremis – they might, just possibly, have been defensible. *American Psycho* appears to be empty of any purpose whatever, other than to get its author back in the news after the critical and commercial failure of his second novel, *Rules of Attraction*.
>
> (ibid.)

Only the author's sense of purpose and commitment to a socio-political critique or to imagining and articulating the limit points of individual and social experience – a commitment somehow made manifest through his writing – could have justified the cruelty and suffering presented in the book. A committed aesthetic, that is, just might have exonerated the narrative of sexual abuse, of murder and bodily dismemberment which threatens to interpellate its readers at regular intervals. Inevitably, then, the failure or absence of that aesthetic turns *American Psycho* into, at worst, a self-aggrandizing and vacuously exploitative or, at best, a failed and derivative exposé of the urban life and times of a serial killer.

Above all, the threat of the absence, or omission, which Hudson discovers in Ellis's novel is its potential for being transferred onto a (mass) readership – a readership overwhelmed by a fictional world which is, above all, 'meaningless': 'Patrick Bateman [the psycho of the title] is a cipher. His friends are ciphers. His victims only come alive when they are dying . . . Ellis doesn't have anything else to say. His characterless, uninflected world is meaningless because he cannot provide a single three-dimensional character to judge it by' (ibid.). Reviewers of *American Psycho* are remarkably consistent on this point. Compare 'Bookworm' in *Punch*:

> Bret Easton Ellis may have intended to criticize the greedy and uncaring society of rich New York, but he has ended up a prime example of it. Just as Patrick Bateman has to keep killing more cruelly and more often to stimulate himself, so Bret Easton Ellis

has continually to keep going a step further. The reader's sensitivity to cruelty is steadily numbed, not enhanced by this process.

('Bookworm' 1991)

Similarly, John Heilpern, writing for the *Independent*, suggested that *American Psycho* failed as a 'send-up of Yuppie consumerism' because it reads 'like an endless brand-name catalogue, thereby combining shopping with killing' (Heilpern 1990: 11). Thus *American Psycho* is both scandalous and repulsive because we do not feel what we are supposed to feel when we read it and we don't feel what we should because the narrative itself fails to make the proper distinctions between right and wrong, between shopping and killing, between being dead and being alive: 'His victims only come alive when they are dying.'

Responses like these are familiar and compelling, apparently inseparable from any public critique of representations of violence and brutality. The charge of desensitization, in particular, has a force in relation to *American Psycho* that it sometimes lacks elsewhere. Crudely, the 'endless brand-name catalogue' which accounts for the bulk of its narrative is so unremittingly tedious that there is a sense of relief when something happens – a relief, difficult not to call perverse, that is then caught out in its participation in a narrative event almost invariably embroiled in a more or less sickening and sexualized form of murderousness. Occasionally, as I suggested in the discussion of the degraded spectatorship associated with the 'brat pack' cinema, it is caught out in a shared joke, in a type of black humour which, if only because it is recognizable, finds its audience:

> Jeanette's dilemma lies outside my definition of guilt, and I had told her, truthfully, over dinner that it was very hard for me to express concern for her that I don't feel. During the entire drive from my place on the Upper West Side, she's been sobbing. The only clear, identifiable emotion coming from her is desperation and maybe longing, and though I successfully ignore her for most of the ride I finally have to tell her, 'Listen, I've already taken two Xanax this morning so, uh, you're incapable of, like upsetting me.'
>
> (Ellis 1991: 381)

It is this kind of recognition which makes a reading of *American Psycho* so unsettling and, at the same time, so unstable. There is an affect (or even affects) produced through reading the book – not least through that juxtaposition of a low-key, 'out-of-it' humour and the more unreadable, in a strong sense, scenes – but it does not fall easily into the categories of anguish and commitment, outrage and pleasure, most immediately available to the critics of the book and its readers. Given this uncertainty, Hudson's description, or dismissal, of Ellis's readers as 'apologists' overlooks one of the more complex aspects of the book: the different reading strategies it seems to demand, from bored inattention to absorption, from anticipatory skimming to sickness, from a mechanical registering of those brand-names to a kind of reading with eyes closed. In this sense, by suggesting that the reader who doesn't accuse the book is apologizing for it, Hudson locks the narrative and its consumer into precisely the scene of accusation and defence that the novel is charged with having omitted – a profoundly melancholic scene which stages a set of questions: who is to blame? Whose fault is it? Is it Ellis who should never have written this book or his readers who shouldn't read it?

The possibility that a reader is faced with the difficulty of not knowing what to think or do about a writing which represents, but seems to be without, trauma is disallowed here – along with the difficulty of not knowing what to do with a suffering that seems to be without the anguished purpose, even without the pleasure, which would locate the book, both more and less problematically, either within a committed aesthetic or within the confines of hard-core porn. Beyond that generic certainty, beyond the scene of accusation and retribution, beyond perverse pleasure and its guilt, there is a form of bewilderment which seems to derive as much from what doesn't have a place in Ellis's narratives as from what does. This type of omission and bewilderment can be used to make the link between Ellis's fiction and the apparent loss of symbolization in Milpitas. Further, we can read Ellis's first novel, *Less Than Zero*, published six years before *American Psycho*, for its exemplary inflection of that omission through the act of 'just looking'. There are three key episodes in the novel which present a decision to look or not to look at a scene or object marked as intolerable as the measure of youthful disaffection. Back in LA for the Christmas holidays, the narrator, Clay, falls in with a habitual round of shopping, parties, drug taking, rock clubs and sex. He engages, or not, in *non sequitur* conversations with parents and friends and visits his psychiatrist who has an idea for making a film. Being out of it on the novel's invested drugs – valium, thorazine, downers and heroin – contributes to the inertia characterizing the relationships between Clay and his friends. The first 'look' takes place at one of their parties:

> Everyone in the room is looking up at a large television screen. I look up to the screen. There's a young girl, nude, maybe fifteen, on a bed, her arms tied together above her head and her legs spread apart, each foot tied to a bedpost. She's lying on what looks like newspaper . . . The camera cuts quickly to a young, thin, nude, scared-looking boy, sixteen, maybe seventeen, being pushed into the room by this fat black guy, who's also naked and who's got this huge hardon. The boy stares at the camera for an uncomfortably long time, this panicked expression on his face. The black man ties the boy up on the floor, and I wonder why there's a chainsaw in the corner of the room, in the background, and then has sex with him and he has sex with the girl and then walks off the screen. When he comes back he's carrying a box. It looks like a toolbox and I'm confused for a minute and Blair walks out of the room. And he takes out an ice pick and what looks like a wire hanger and a package of nails and then a thin, large knife and he comes toward the girl and Daniel smiles and nudges me in the ribs. I leave quickly as the black man tries to push a nail into the girl's neck.
>
> (Ellis 1985: 153)

This passage signals the limit of what it is tolerable to watch with a look that, initially communal, is soon fragmented by what is taking place on the screen. Ten boys stay in the room, Blair (Clay's nominal girlfriend) leaves, Daniel smiles, Clay leaves 'quickly' but remains within earshot: 'But someone's turned the volume up . . . I listen to the sound of the trees shuffling in the warm wind and the screams of a young girl coming from the television' (ibid.: 153–4). Both narrator and reader, then, become spectators of a murderous, sexual image through a reference to the conventional cinematic technique for catching out the viewer in his or her own voyeurism – the boy stares into the camera for an uncomfortably long time. At the same time, the look is sanctioned insofar as it is mistaken or accidental: Clay's look is uncertain, he does not know what he is looking at and he leaves the moment pornography is transformed into snuff. That transformation then generates a question about what is real, about the authenticity of what the camera has filmed – real or fake sex, real or fake torture, real or fake death. The case for the film's genuineness is made, almost comically, via an appeal to castration: '"I mean, like, how can you fake a castration? They cut the balls off that guy real slowly. You can't fake that," the boy says' (ibid.: 154). The privileged narcissistic object, it seems, can be put into circulation, at the very moment of its brutal loss, to ensure that the representation of that loss on film is innocent of fictionalizing. In other words, at its most guilty moment, representation is at least innocent of fictionalizing, an innocence which then doubles the guilt of the spectator who wants to see the worst of the 'real thing', who cannot make do with fiction.

Thus: 'I sit there and the need to see the worst washes over me, quickly, eagerly' (ibid.: 175). Clay is watching a friend forced into homosexual prostitution to feed a drug habit. He is there simply as the spectator of the client's fantasies, as the one who just looks – '"One just to watch, of course"', as Julian's pimp explains (ibid.: 169). As spectator, Clay is positioned by the client, a middle-aged business man '"into real estate, son"', who 'shifts his gaze from Julian over to me, to make sure that I'm watching':

> The man sits me down in an easy chair and positions me nearer the bed and then, satisfied, walks up to Julian and places his hand on Julian's bare shoulder. His hand drops down to Julian's jockey shorts and Julian closes his eyes.
>
> 'You're a very nice young man.'
>
> An image of Julian in fifth grade, kicking a soccer ball across a green field.
>
> 'Yes, you're a very beautiful boy,' the man from Indiana says, 'and here, that's all that matters.'
>
> Julian opens his eyes and stares into mine and I turn away and notice a fly buzzing lazily over to the wall next to the bed. I wonder what the man and Julian are going to do. I tell myself I could leave. I could simply say to the man from Muncie and Julian that I want to leave. But, again, the words don't, can't, come out and I sit there and the need to see the worst washes over me, quickly, eagerly.
>
> (ibid.: 175)

Clay doesn't close his eyes for the five hours that they're in the hotel room – until the memory of Julian at school 'doesn't disturb me anymore' (ibid.: 177). But he starts to worry that perhaps his father knows this man who is also a husband and a father: 'I keep wondering if my father knows this guy. I try to shake the thought from my head, the idea of this guy maybe coming up to my father at Ma Maison or Trumps, but it stays there, stuck' (ibid.: 174). It sticks, along with the fear that he will see his father's business card amongst those in the man's wallet, reinforcing a sense that, for this novel, the father cannot be kept apart from the pimp or the trick. '"Now, you know that you're my best boy and you know that I care for you. Just like my own kid. Just like my own son"' Julian's pimp tells him at the same time as he pumps him full of drugs and sends him off to the man from Muncie (ibid.: 171). And the man from Muncie, who carries photographs of his wife and sons in his wallet, still buys boys – one to rape and one to watch; or more precisely one to participate in, by looking at, the assaults on Julian who, the narrator tells us, is constantly closing his eyes and 'trying to smile', his victimization doubled by the presence of an onlooker he has described as a friend (ibid.: 176).

At this point, the guilt of the father refuses Pye's reading of *Less Than Zero* as a 'warning' to parents because the parents – as producers and consumers of the book's economic and cultural milieu – are themselves so very much a part of the disaffection and perversity which, in a generous reading, this novel could be said to critique. That disaffection and perversity accumulates through the looking which structures the novel (including a communal look at a dead boy in an alley) and could be said to culminate in the scene which Clay finally refuses to watch – a 12-year-old girl, drugged and tied up, about to be gang-raped by the young men in Rip's apartment:

Spin puts a tape on and then takes off his shirt and then his jeans. He has a hardon and he pushes it at the girl's lips and then looks over at us. 'You can watch if you want.'
I leave the room.
Rip follows me.
'Why?' is all I ask Rip.
'What?'
'Why, Rip?'
Rip looks confused. 'Why that? You mean in there?'
I try to nod.
'Why not? What the hell?'
'Oh, God, Rip, come on, she's eleven.'
'Twelve,' Rip corrects.
'Yeah, twelve,' I say, thinking about it for a moment.
'Hey, don't look at me like I'm some sort of scumbag or something. I'm not.'
I lean up against the wall. I can hear Spin moaning in the bedroom and then the sound of a hand slapping maybe a face.

'But you don't need anything. You have everything,' I tell him.
Rip looks at me. 'No, I don't.'
'What?'
'No, I don't.'
There's a pause and then I ask, 'Oh, shit, Rip, what don't you have?'
'I don't have anything to lose.'

(ibid.: 188–9)

The gang rape of the young girl signals the limit of what Clay will watch but not the limit of what the reader is asked to look at. Clay doesn't say anything, just leaves the apartment – another 'silence' that, for Greil Marcus, situates the novel within a postmodern 'anti-terrain', within a 'yes, endlessly diffused' (Marcus 1985: 12). It's a strange 'yes' that functions as negativity rather than 'not no' and it speaks the impossibility of finding a position from which to object, from which to say no. It is accompanied by a turn to memory as Clay recalls a story he has been told about a summer party that 'somehow got out of hand' (Ellis 1985: 191). A young girl from San Diego was raped, murdered and mutilated. In effect, this memory – or this narrative of a memory – *screens* what is taking place in Rip's apartment, both running through and displaying what is happening, or may happen, to the girl in Rip's bedroom *and* making it disappear, turning it into something that has already happened and so cannot be changed. It is, I think, remarkable that this move is made when the narrative confronts itself with a demand for an answer to the question: 'why?' On the one hand, in Rip's bleakly trite response to that 'why?' – 'I don't have anything to lose' – there is something like an appeal to the same 'surface knowingness and playfulness' of the popular postmodern that we saw in the final frames of *Ferris Bueller's Day Off* (Creed 1988: 97). Certainly, Marcus assimilates the novel to a postmodern ethic and aesthetic on the basis of a type of nothing to lose or 'fin-de-siècle malaise': 'The things that go on in this book lack the apocalyptic aura of the Manson crimes; this is fin-de-siècle stuff' (Marcus 1985: 12). While the protagonists in *Less Than Zero* watch snuff movies, he notes ambiguously, Manson had them made. That is, people of the 1960s 'did it'; those in the 1980s just look at it – another historical shift between the 1960s and the 1980s mediated, this time, by a different kind of murderous aggression. But, on the other hand, in its ambivalent turn to the past and so to a memory that stands in for the present, for what is happening and what could be done if only the place could be found from which to say 'no' to obscenity, *Less Than Zero* could also be said to question, or at least to enact, a logic of omission which is internal to a melancholic fantasy of having nothing to lose and its very ambiguous sense that something else might have been.

A LOGIC OF OMISSION

We can start to clarify this through three different psychoanalytic schemas of memory and loss. In *Studies on Hysteria*, Freud notes that Frau Emmy von N. 'had got into the habit of stammering and clacking whenever she was frightened' and that 'these symptoms had come to be attached not solely to the initial traumas, but to a long train of memories associated with them, which I had omitted to wipe out' (*PFL* 3: 133). This is a difficult moment for the history of psychoanalysis not only because there is something insupportable about the idea of obliterating a woman's memory but because elsewhere Freud insisted that nothing in the psyche ever goes away. Thus the loss that falls away, that doesn't 'happen', contorts the relation between the unconscious and the social and subject identity based on the repression and sublimation of drives, a loss and a contortion which are reminiscent of the shock of Milpitas where something went missing and opened up the space between two deaths, the biological and the symbolic death – a space inhabited by the body of a woman. Something more than anxiety attaches to that space, something more like what Hanna Segal calls psychotic terror, a fear not of one death, not even one's own, but of the death of the world (Segal 1987). In fact, references to a generation 'hardened in an age of nuclear war' (*The Los Angeles Times*, 27 November 1981) suggest that the end of the world was never far away as an explanation for the students' apparent failure to mourn a friend, a failure which could be said to have become a form of symbolic murder anticipating what Jacques Derrida has called the 'loss of the archive' – the fundamental threat of the nuclear imagination when no social remainder is left to remember and to mourn (Derrida 1984: 28).

When social mourning fails, when friendship fails, are we then up against a different kind of unconscious – an unconscious that guarantees neither an individual nor a social identity because things can always go missing? We can perhaps start to clarify this question through the possibility of a radical loss which structures Freud's account of friendship and of mourning in a few pages on 'Affects in

Dreams' in *The Interpretation of Dreams*. That account returns almost obsessively to both the fantasy and the real event of losing a friend. In this case, the friend is a nephew, a year older than Freud, who plays the role of both 'friend and opponent':

> I have already shown how my warm friendships as well as my enmities with contemporaries went back to my relations in childhood with a nephew who was a year my senior . . . All my friends have in a certain sense been reincarnations of this first figure . . . they have been *revenants* . . . This last group of thoughts was connected once again with the intermediate thought in the latent content of the dream from which the associative paths diverged in contrary directions: 'No one is irreplaceable!' 'There are nothing but *revenants*: all those we have lost come back!'
>
> (*PFL* 4: 622–6)

Because the friend is always both friend and opponent, the *revenant* negotiates both aggression and loss – proof that aggression does not amount to absolute destruction and that loss, following the course of what Freud would later describe as 'true mourning', can always be overcome by finding a new object, by consigning 'memories and expectations' attached to the lost object to the past (*PFL* 11: 253). At the same time, this is a past which keeps coming back, which keeps things circulating even as it seems to lose them because nothing, and nobody, ever really goes away. The friend is a double, a substitute, even a compensation, a key figure in the development of the classical account of the unconscious associated with the mechanisms of repression and substitutive sublimation. But this psychical economy can be set against a mechanism of omission sketched out in Freud's letters at the time of his daughter Sophie's death in 1920. The dominant issue here is forgetting. In Freud's case, as Derrida notes in his extensive commentary on these letters, it is the 'definitive *Fortgehen*' of the 'favourite daughter' that has to be forgotten (all citations from Freud's letters are taken from Derrida 1987: 329–30). Far from finding a substitute for her, Freud writes that it is 'as if she had never been' and her loss is a 'loss to be forgotten'. This drive toward forgetting, deriving, Freud tells Ferenczi, from an 'irreparable narcissistic injury', is at odds with the painstaking work of mourning outlined in 'Mourning and Melancholia' a few years before as well as the apparently unshakeable faith in the *revenant* so evident twenty years earlier. Moreover, the desire to forget resonates with the violence of a second killing, the symbolic erasure of the daughter following her biological death – 'as if she had never been'.

Freud's 'forgetting' his daughter suggests a reading of an unconscious which is not governed – which is not able to be governed – by the eternal return of the lost object in the guise of someone else; 'forgetting', refusing or being unable to bear to remember traces another no less fantasmatic logic of having had nothing to lose in the first place. The loss of the daughter, who perhaps can never be a friend, could be said to have produced a memory of what has never been, the memory of a loss which has never 'happened'. This contortion of memory recalls Nicholas Abraham and Maria Torok's rereading of the case history of the Wolf Man and their description of the subject who carries an unavowable secret loss, a cryptic subject who lives a 'trapped' or tantalized life in which the ego is constantly on the lookout for witnesses to what has happened and yet constantly refuses, or is unable, to say what it is (Abraham and Torok 1986: esp. 3–40). *The Wolf Man's Magic Word* presents the case history of the Wolf Man in the context of Abraham and Torok's reworking of Freud's theory of melancholia as the symptom of a denial of a 'real' injury or loss (a denial which tends to make the concept of melancholia central to an account of the 'failure' to respond). Abraham and Torok read this denial as the effect of a fantasy of having nothing to lose which protects against the knowledge of an unbearable loss. At the same time, they extend the analysis of melancholic fantasy by situating it as the effect of a wish to protect the prestige and the desire of an ideal object whose loss is inextricably related to its failing and its shame – a shame and a failing which must, at all costs, be kept secret.

Thus something has been lost that was narcissistically indispensable – because it was playing the role of an ideal for the ego – and, as such, its loss cannot for one moment be acknowledged. At this point where the prestige of the object and the subject's own narcissism intersect, the subject can be possessed by somebody else's desire to protect their own idealized status – a possession which may also clarify both the type of identification and masquerade discussed in Chapter 2 and the spectator tantalized into making an exorbitant, sometimes even suicidal, demand for love on the screen. Abraham and Torok describe this possession as a form of self-to-self hysteria, or preservative repression, in which not the subject but the other's desire is at stake, in which the subject is preoccupied not by his or her unconscious desire but by someone else's – by someone else's fantasy (Abraham and Torok 1980; 1986). That internal drama then sets up the conditions both for the production of a memory of what has never been (for the subject) and for a failure to register a 'real event', for an event to pass 'straight through' the psyche because the 'subject' – subject to the preservation of someone else's desire – is not there for the event to happen to her or him.

What Abraham and Torok are saying here is suggestive in the context of the preoccupied, tantalized and idealizing identifications that have been emerging through the different readings of cinema and spectatorship put forward in this book. There is also a link to be made with Donald Winnicott's distinction between a tantalizing and a deficient environment and their different effects on the development of a capacity for symbolization. The distinction is set out in 'Fear of Breakdown', published in 1986 in an attempt to account precisely for the effects of what doesn't happen and for a subject that has never been present either to itself or to its world:

> To understand this, it is necessary to think not of trauma but of nothing happening when something might profitably have happened. It is easier for a patient to remember trauma than to remember nothing happening when it might have happened. At the time, the patient did not know what might have happened, and so could not experience anything except to note that something might have been.
>
> (Winnicott 1986: 180)

Winnicott describes this tantalization as 'perhaps the worst thing that can happen to a human baby', a worst against which even a psychotic defence is unsuccessful (ibid.: 176). If there is a certain liberation from anxiety in this state, he suggests, it is only in exchange for a primitive agony – agony because 'anxiety is not a strong enough word here' – and a different type of unconscious:

> The unconscious here is not exactly the repressed unconscious of psychoneurosis, nor is it the unconscious of Freud's formulation of the part of the psyche that is very close to neurophysiological functioning. Nor is it the unconscious of Jung's which I would call: all those things that go on in underground caves, or (in other words) the world's mythology . . . In this special context the unconscious means that the ego integration is not able to encompass something. The ego is too immature to gather all phenomena into the area of personal omnipotence.
>
> (ibid.: 177)

This failure of a capacity for omnipotence – no less essential because it is fantasmatic – underlies both the subject's fear of breakdown and his or her search for 'the past detail which is *not yet experienced*' and which takes the form of 'a looking for this detail in the future' (ibid.). The psychoanalytic work demanded by this unconscious is not a lifting of repression but a strange kind of remembering of something that both has and hasn't happened: 'This detail is already a fact' and the analysand 'needs to "remember" this but it is not possible to remember something that has not yet happened, and this thing of the past has not happened yet because the patient was not there for it to happen to' (ibid.: 179). The wager of both this remembering and Winnicott's psychoanalysis here is not only the ego's appropriation of its experience in the here and now of the treatment but also a negotiation of something like a fantasy of having nothing to lose, a fantasy which starts from a difficult but necessary acceptance of psychical death:

> I now understand for the first time what my schizophrenic patient (who did kill herself) meant when she said: 'All I ask you to do is to help me to commit suicide for the right reason instead of for the wrong reason.' I did not succeed and she killed herself in despair of finding the solution. Her aim (as I now see) was to get it stated by me that she died in early infancy.
>
> (ibid.: 179–80)

On the one hand, this is close to Julia Kristeva's analysis of the exchange between the 'borderline personality' and a maternal abjection which produces neither love nor psychic life (Kristeva 1987). On the other hand, and very schematically, the different economies of omission sketched out here – the dispossession which produces a form of death-in-life – start to shift one influential contemporary account of the psychical type most often called upon to describe and to explain the kind of symbolic omission which seemed to be taking place in Milpitas; that is, the 'postmodern' psyche precisely, as deficient, fragmented, 'bereft' of knowledge, body and of feeling, including anxiety. What Fredric Jameson has described as the postmodern 'liberation from anxiety . . . from every other kind of feeling as well, since there is no longer a self present to do the feeling' (Jameson 1984: 64) is reinflected, through the different schemas put forward by Abraham and Torok and Donald Winnicott, as a liberation which exchanges anxiety for agony and for the loss internal to a profoundly painful sense that something might have been. Thus the dissociation of Ellis's novels, the silent and apparently dissociated looking at the body of a murdered woman in Milpitas, may be assimilable not, or not only, to a pervasive voyeurism which prefers to look at rather than live in the real world, but to a melancholic misery that unable to be acknowledged, let alone resolved, can only be turned back on itself.

LOOKING BEYOND THE PALE

The 'just looking' and saying nothing which takes place through *Less Than Zero* points to an intimate connection between the loss of symbolization and the dissociated or affectless looking beyond the pale which made Milpitas – and then *River's Edge* – infamous. A more general point can be made, too, that one of the most challenging aspects of contemporary cinema is its necessary engagement with public anxiety about the anomic effects of this type of 'just looking' and the cumulative effects of cinema itself. *River's Edge* confronts that anxiety by situating itself somewhere between the youth cult and teen violence films – Jonathan Kaplan's *Over the Edge* (1979 – scripted by Tim Hunter), Coppola's *Rumble Fish* and *The Outsiders* (1983), Penelope Spheeris's *Suburbia* (1983) and *The Boys Next Door* (1985) – and *The Accused*, directed by Kaplan nearly ten years after *Over the Edge*. Firmly within a cinematic tradition which turns the victimized body of the woman into the body of cinema, the relation of *The Accused*, for example, to its own images of the woman raised the perhaps undecidable issue of whether the film lines up on the side of exploitation or ethics – of whether the explicit images of rape, suspended throughout but finally included at the end of the film, subverted its efforts to criminalize the men who looked at as well as (or instead of) the men who actually committed a gang rape.[2] In one sense, *The Accused* literalizes the criminality of spectatorship – what the spectator sees, the sexualized aggression of a gang rape, underlines the potential violence of any spectacle and any spectatorship. At the same time, the passivity of the spectator is put into question by the film's refusal to accept a simple distinction between 'just looking' and doing, between looking and causing something to happen. That indistinction turns looking into a trial and binds it to a law which may, at any moment, demand to know where we stand, whose side we are on, whether we are going to speak or not. The conclusion of *The Accused*, in fact, turns the spectator who will finally say what he has seen into a 'true' witness, a hero, whose look at the woman *in extremis* is legitimized by his recourse to the law.

Similarly, *River's Edge* questions the collective dimension of spectatorship in cinema by foregrounding a failure of social identification through the issues of spectatorship and culpability in relation to a look at the body of a dead woman. But, unlike *The Accused*, *River's Edge* does not manage to produce the category of the true witness within the narrative of the film, a failure which may be taken back both to its more direct reference to a real event and to its engagement with youth disaffection, with the 'new type of kid'. The film opens with an androgynous young boy, Tim, throwing his sister's doll into the river. On the other side of the river, John, a high school student, sits howling beside the naked body of the girl he has just strangled. At school, John tells his gang that he has killed Jamie and, thinking he's joking, they go to check on the body. Layne, the group's speed-freak, treats the murder as a test of the friends' loyalty to one another (another gendered loyalty) but most of the group seem too unsure or unconcerned either to conceal the body or to contact the police. Even John is so uninterested that Layne ends up rolling the body into the river himself. Meanwhile, Matt, the film's nominal hero, has told the police what he knows. Back home he fights with both his flower-power mother's boyfriend and with Tim, the younger brother, who threatens to kill him for having 'narked' on John. Meanwhile, discovering the police waiting for John outside his home, Layne arranges for him to hide with Feck. A sixties drop-out and recluse for twenty years since shooting his girlfriend, Feck lives with Ellie, a sex doll, and supplies the local teenagers with free dope. Reluctant to tell Layne that he has turned John in, Matt spends the night in a park with another member of the gang, Clarissa. As dawn breaks on the second day, they are woken by the sound of a gunshot. Feck has shot John and discarded Ellie in the river. That morning, the students are harangued for their lack of feeling by a representative of the radical 1960s counterculture, a teacher who belonged, as he puts it, to the generation that took to the streets and made a difference. The gang decides to take the day off and go down to the river. There they discover John's body and Tim turns up, having broken into Feck's and stolen his gun. He threatens to shoot Matt, who manages to dissuade him by appealing to the fact that they are brothers. Feck, meanwhile, is in hospital (having been knocked out by Tim and his friend), explaining that he had to shoot John because he was without feeling for the girl he had killed. The film ends with Jamie's funeral and the gang looking, one by one, into the open casket.

In an interview published in *Monthly Film Bulletin* in 1987, Tim Hunter discussed the impact of *River's Edge* in terms of the film's engagement with a traumatic social and political reality:

> I enjoy it when I talk to actual journalists, not movie critic journalists, but crime reporters. Quite a few have said to me, based on their years at the hall of justice, that they thought *River's Edge* was the most accurate portrayal of juvenile crime. That makes me feel good because those guys have experience; they've actually seen and dealt with people. They don't put a filter between themselves and the world . . . There is a sense of hopelessness. Traditionally, this has been a society which the people always felt that they could change. But we're in a very difficult, very entrenched time now, and it trickles down very easily to a bunch of stoner kids in suburban communities in Anytown, U.S.A. They just assume that the bomb is going to drop, and they couldn't care less about school, and so they don't see past the moment in their lives. I suppose what the film is saying is that you can't draw the Stanley Kramer lines any more . . . It's going to take a real reorientation of social priorities . . . I felt that *River's Edge* would be serving some kind of moral function just by being an eye-opener.
>
> (Hunter 1987: 295–6)

A clear moral function is assigned to the camera here. It is to be an 'eye-opener', to force more looking but, this time, from a dangerous and affected place since, according to Hunter, 'there's no comfortable viewpoint from which you can watch the film and think, "Well, I'm safe from this"' (ibid.: 296). Like Pye, Hunter is uneasy with the idea of just looking but he does not suggest that we should not look at all; instead, looking itself has to be made traumatic so that the spectator is forced into the role of witness or delegate for the community. This recalls Lacan's description of the role of the Chorus of a Greek tragedy: 'Even if you do not feel anything, the Chorus will do so in your place' (Lacan, cited in Žižek 1989: 35). That is, there is a radically exterior aspect to even the most intimate of affects and an absolutely social dimension to looking. The moral wager of *River's Edge*, then, is to effect a rehabilitation of the spectator, to force him or her into the work of symbolization that might start to re-elaborate the social bond which, along with affect, along with mourning, has disappeared.

In 'The Question Oshima', Stephen Heath recalls Bazin's fascination with a shot of Yvonne de Bray from *Les Parents Terribles*: 'The object of the shot is not what she is looking at, not even her look; it is *looking at her looking*.' Heath goes on to suggest that the cinematic apparatus is the 'machinery for the fiction of such a position, for the totalising security of looking at looking and at "her"' (Heath 1981: 148). But, as has been suggested in different ways throughout this book, there may also be a beyond of that totalizing security. On the one hand, the spectator is fascinated by what he or she is looking at, caught up in the imaginary fiction of omnipotence. On the other hand, following the logic of the 'looking at looking' described by Heath, the spectator is subject to the paranoid question internal to that fiction: 'Am I being looked at by someone else?' 'Looking at looking' doubles both the potential for a fascination secure in the knowledge that the object being looked at is looking elsewhere – and will *not* look back – and the paranoia, the anxiety, essential to the knowledge that if I am able to look at somebody looking without them seeing me, then my looking itself can become the object of a look from elsewhere that I can know nothing about. *River's Edge* uses this potential internal to looking in relation to its own most controversial image: the image of a dead woman, so inseparable from voyeurism in cinema, becomes a key element in the film's function as an eye-opener supposed to shock the spectator into ethics. At the same time, the image of the woman which runs through the film could be described (or dismissed) as one more exemplary instance of the way in which the body of the woman becomes the body of cinema, invested both by the film text and the discursive practices of the cinematic institution. While Tim Hunter appeals to that image to provoke some kind of change, one reading of the production and distribution history of the film suggests it may have helped to secure a certain box office return. The producers of *River's Edge*, Midge Sanford and Sarah Pillsbury, took Neal Jiminez's script in 1983, after it had been turned down by all the major studios, and approached the independents for backing. Sarah Pillsbury has commented: 'We tried to interest them by saying, "There's a naked dead girl"' (cited in Combs 1987: 294). Thus the image of the dead girl became the selling point of the script, supposed – both remarkably and predictably – to deflect from its bleakness by 'going for the jugular', to quote Russell Schwartz of Island (cited in Harmetz 1987: 9).

It is, I think, a mark of the film's achievement that it constantly replays that image while, at the same time, remaining very resistant to a simple charge of voyeurism. Apparently courting the accusation that it is turning the body into a peepshow, the (sometimes unmotivated) camera returns to the dead girl by the river throughout the first half of the film. This looking – the camera's, the spectator's – is, however, disturbed when Matt is finally questioned by a police officer about how and what he felt when he saw the dead girl. The officer asks how the 'sight of this dead body' affected him – 'Did it anger, sadden, or please you in any way?' These questions, and Matt's repeated 'I dunno' are voiced over the discovery of Jamie's body in the river, over the image of the dead girl on screen, so that the question – 'Did the sight please you?' – implicates not only Matt's viewing, or the group's viewing, of the body as part of the film narrative but also our looking, the sight of the body on film. In other words, the image which is used to solicit the look is used to turn that look back onto the spectator who is thereby invoked as something akin to a guilty witness. We are forced by the questions put to Matt, and so to us, to see ourselves seeing in a way that suggests we are being 'apprehended' as we see, that a look is coming from elsewhere in order to make us answerable. The very interest in the image, then, becomes the means by which the film can start to counteract the omission that is its object, to construct the symbolic – through something like shame or guilt – which seems to be lacking.

'Start to' because, as the film moves from the look at the dead girl by the river to the look at her in an open casket at her funeral, it is by no means clear that *River's Edge* can really make the difference. This uncertainty becomes the film's overwhelming question: Not only how do you make a difference but how do you tell the difference – between a doll and a woman, between the psychotic and the normal, between a murderer and a friend? Again, something about the troubling coincidence between the look courted in the hills outside Milpitas and the look in the cinema is at stake here. The attempt to rehabilitate or to repair the look produces the spectator as guilty, as mournful, only insofar as *River's Edge* refuses or fails to secure a difference between cinematic and social spectatorship, between the looking that happens in cinema and the looking which took place in Milpitas. To put this slightly differently, *River's Edge* exposes the way that a cinematically specific kind of looking cannot be contained within that cinema, an exposure which puts enormous pressure both on our models of representation and spectatorship and on the ethical potential, or oppositional stance, available to cinema as such: crudely, if looks can kill, how can looking effect a cure? To put this another way: on the one hand, *River's Edge* fulfils Hunter's claims both by forcing a closer look at 'what happened' and by dispersing the look at the dead body to include all the potential spectators of the film. We are refused any easy condemnation of the students in Milpitas by being forced away from what Hunter described as the Stanley Kramer lines. On the other hand, we start to lose any way of referring to what, if anything, is different about looking at a 'real' dead body, a loss which seems to re-enact the failure to symbolize the murder which was so central to the trauma in the first place. This problem remains even if looking in cinema is made different from looking outside it by theorizing cinematic representation not as a reflection but as a fashioning, or fictioning, of reality. Once again the film will have repeated, or at least reinforced, one of key elements of the trauma of non-symbolization – the failure to take murder seriously enough. Once again, as soon as we start to represent, to fictionalize, a 'real' death, something of its reality goes missing. Thus *River's Edge* reveals an impasse in which the act of representation, of symbolization, is laid open to the accusation that it betrays the spectator into the very dereliction it aims to dispel – and presents that impasse so acutely, perhaps, because the film itself is caught up in the work of symbolizing a failure of symbolization. It is as if the representation of a failure of representation doubles the demand for regret and reparation – for more mournful representation – and doubles it again when the film, through Tim Hunter's appeal to its moral function, is drawn into the logic of cinema as cure.

There is also something uncanny about the way in which the disputes about the exhibition of *River's Edge* in Milpitas provoke another form of repetition of the real event. One of the students who kept quiet about the murder in 1981 was interviewed for an article on *River's Edge* and its reception in Milpitas, published in *Newsweek* in 1986. He insisted that the town was incapable of forgetting: '"They don't know what to do, so they try to block it out," he said. "That's what I try to do – act like it didn't happen. But it just keeps coming back."' Another teenager commented: '"All I knew was that something happened up in the hills. It was so hush-hush. If you said anything, adults would say, 'Don't talk about it, it's a bad thing.' That only made it worse"' (Abramson 1987: 25). The oscillation between remembering and forgetting, between trying to forget and only being able to remember, between wanting to know and finding only others' desire not to know, is, perhaps, what is finally at issue in the public dismissal of *River's Edge* as 'sick'. Prevented from seeing the film by the town's ban and confronted by their parents' refusal to talk about 'it', teenagers from Milpitas travelled to the cinemas in nearby San José to see the film. In other words, the effects of the first loss of symbolization appear to have become eminently transferable, initiating a collective repetition in the form of another decision not to say anything (which maps the students' omission onto the parents) and, more distressing perhaps, not to allow anything to be said or shown – a prohibition which forces the 'illegitimate' look in cinema outside the town.

It is precisely this tendency to transfer and to repeat the trauma it represents which has generated critical unease with *River's Edge*. Commenting on its apparent refusal to comment, Judith Williamson notes that the film itself 'gives us very little to respond to (apart from the body of a girl we didn't know) and the viewer is left as affectless as the kids appear to be' (Williamson 1987: 21). Again, it is a question of whether or not *River's Edge* can really make the difference, a question which always returns to the representation of the dead girl. Critics have picked up on the way that the film trafficks a certain indistinction between John's strangling Jamie and Tim's throwing his sister's doll into the river – an indistinction then quite easily read as a symptom of the 'moral quicksand' that *River's Edge* inevitably falls into (Simon 1987: 55). Aljean Harmetz suggests that the students 'respond to their friend's murder as if she were simply a doll', underlining the way in which the parallels set up between John and Tim risk symbolizing the loss of a doll and the death of a woman as the same thing (Harmetz 1987:9). But Harmetz is appealing to a symbolic system that is disrupted, if not inoperative, throughout the film. Dolls and women *are* distinguished in this film and distinguished decisively according to whether their loss is mourned or not. Dolls, and not dead women, are mourned; they're mourned because they are friends. Missy, the doll thrown away by Tim, is given a ritual burial by Matt and his younger sister; Ellie, the sex doll, described by the students as Feck's girlfriend and by Feck himself as his friend, is symptomatic not, or not only, of a perverse sexuality but of a problem about what it means to have a friend – a problem to which the film returns almost obsessively through Feck. It is also indicative of the confusion introduced into the category of the friend by *River's Edge* that, when Feck mourns the loss of a 'good friend today' at its close, we don't know whether he's referring to John, to Ellie or to his gun. Each one has been called a good friend and then shot, discarded or stolen in the last few sequences of the film.

Crucially, this disturbance frames the film's appeal to the body of the dead woman to secure a bond of friendship. A young woman's death becomes the test of group loyalty, and a consensus that, as a woman, she 'had it coming' because 'women are evil, man' organizes the exchange between the gang and Feck. Similarly, Tim tries to join his older brother's gang with an offer to 'show you a dead body'. In effect, the film is putting a dead woman into exchange in a way that skews a more familiar account of the social tie as the effect of the exchange of women in marriage – an exchange between men which produces the socializing taboo against incest and the relation between brothers-in-law. In Claude Lévi-Strauss's classic structural analysis of the social bond, for example, the socializing relation between brothers-in-law is the result of a complementary alliance established through the woman who becomes the image of difference *between* men as well as different *to* men. The man who exchanges her is twice the man he was before because now he has a male partner like, but not too like, himself as well as an individual and social identity secured through the woman's difference as object rather than subject of exchange (Lévi-Strauss 1949). But that alliance is obviously disrupted if the woman is dead – as Fred Pfeil points out when, following Gayle Rubin's famous essay on Lévi-Strauss, he finds what he calls the film's 'brutal traffic in women' unable to secure the social bonds tendered over her death (Pfeil 1989: 215; Rubin 1975). Killing a woman, looking at the body of a dead woman, cannot make you a brother or a friend. Instead the categories of the brother (I will come back to this) and of the friend become, at once, increasingly invested and unstable. At its most extreme moment, the narrative collapses the figure of the murderer into that of the friend when Feck, having just promised to be John's friend, shoots him. In one sense, the stepping up of aggression against the woman has destroyed the fragile possibility of ever forging the social tie through her (exchangeable) body. In this sense, again, a dead woman can only symbolize, and that only temporarily, the difference between being dead and being alive – a temporary difference acknowledged in John's response to killing: 'She was lying there dead in front of me and I felt so fucking alive. Funny thing is, I'm dead now. They'll fry me for sure.'

The slide from the exchange of women in marriage to the

exchange of a dead woman can be taken back to the way that the difficulty of sexual difference seems to have given way before, and then become the object of the violence generated by, the impossibility of friendship. To put this another way: the film ends up playing two different logics against one another – a logic of masculine sexual anxiety and a logic of omission which derives from the refusal to call a woman a friend. That sexual anxiety emerges most clearly when the film locates itself in the tradition of Hitchcock and constructs sexual difference through the figure of the woman who should be made to suffer. Carol J. Clover has drawn attention to a comment made by Hitchcock during the filming of *The Birds*: 'I always believe in following the advice of the playwright Sardou. He said "Torture the women!" The trouble today is that we don't torture women enough' (cited in Clover 1989: 111). This tradition is clearly supporting Layne's reassurance to Feck, haunted by the memory of having killed his girlfriend, that 'women are evil, man. You had to kill her.' Further, Hitchcock's *Psycho* serves as a key cinematic reference for *River's Edge* both as a classic of traumatized looking and when the later film harks back to the idea of the 'psycho' – the demonic child, the crazed ex-biker and mother-fixated murderous son.[3] At times, in fact, *River's Edge* virtually insists on the category of the psychotic as an explanation both for the murder it represents and, more generally, for 'what's going wrong'. The attempt to mobilize the group of friends around John, for example, when it bothers to appeal at all, appeals first to the fact that John had his reasons because Jamie was 'shooting her mouth off about his mom', and then to his having a 'couple of loose springs when it comes to his dead mother'. That is, insofar as Norman Bates has to serve as the exemplary cinematic instance of having a 'couple of loose springs' about the mother, there is an attempt to account for the murder as a type of institutional joke. Similarly, the scene in which John tells Feck how he felt about killing a woman positively courts an explanation for the killing in terms of a more or less conventional masculine fear of women's sexuality. John's monologue – spliced, for the first time, with flashbacks to the murder – is then further intercut with shots of Matt and Clarissa, having sex in the park. Clarissa's active sexuality is juxtaposed with Jamie's death while, as he orgasms, Matt is identified with the dying girl, his head falling back at an angle suggesting strangulation. John's speech to Feck is voiced over the two scenes – 'I had total control of her. I wasn't even mad really. I had total control of her' – the voice-over serving both to threaten Clarissa's overt sexual control (she is on top of Matt) and to assimilate the woman's active sexual desire to the man's murderousness.

But, if on one level the film tries to account for John and for murder in terms of a dominant cinematic construction of the psychotic, on another level it cannot maintain the tradition into which it has inserted itself. Perhaps most obviously, while *River's Edge* suggests that John is a voyeur (it is via his look that we spy on Feck dancing with Ellie) and even a necrophile (Jamie's clothes appear to be removed after she has been killed), his perverse or repressed sexuality is not, as such, the issue. John's perversity, if that is what it is, is no enigma; it is not concealed and so it cannot be discovered in order to liberate a curative discourse – whether of psychoanalysis or of *Psycho II* and *III*. As cause, masculine sexual anxiety breaks against what isn't there when John tells Feck: 'I wasn't even mad, really.' But if John wasn't mad, if he wasn't defending either his mother or himself, then the film has a problem explaining what he was doing and why. The displacement of John's guilt onto Tim, the brother who 'drowns' his sister's doll, can be understood as one of the effects of the film's attempt to respond to that problem. (This displacement is not confined to the film – at least one critic has described Tim as the most horrific character of all.) Thus a furious question that could (should?) be put to John – 'Why do you pull shit like that?' – is in fact addressed to Tim, contributing at the same time to the felt indistinction between the death of a woman and the loss of a doll which constantly troubles what could be described as the affective economy of the film. There is also – and we can compare Greil Marcus's discussion of a contemporary malaise – an attempt to represent a historical break between the passion of the 1960s and the apathy of the 1980s in terms of a distinction between two types of psychosis and two kinds of murder. Played by Dennis Hopper, who imports the countercultural and psychotic references of his acting career into this role, Feck, the archetypal sixties casualty, insists that he is not a 'psycho': 'I'm no psycho. I know she's a doll. Right, Ellie?' – a disavowal which only serves to confirm the madness we suspect in him. But the category of the psychotic loses its power of explanation when John, a key representative of a contemporary aggression almost indistinguishable from ennui, willingly and knowingly assumes its name: 'Yeah, I'm a psycho. What other excuse do I have?' Thus there is another 'knowing playfulness' at work here, a playfulness which suspends the explanatory force of the psychotic by using it to map out the difference between two types of murder: the difference between Feck's shooting a woman in the name of love ('I shot a girl once. Put a gun to the back of her head and blew her brains out. I was in love') and John's 'strangling mine' even though she was 'okay'.

The distinction at issue here is between killing for love and killing to feel alive, between feeling too much and not feeling enough. Feck invokes precisely that difference when he tries to explain why he had to kill John: 'I at least loved her [the woman he killed] . . . there was no hope for him. He didn't feel a thing.' It is this appeal to love, to murder as love and love as murder, which then comes to support an unnerving tendency to invest Feck as the film's 'moral centre' (Powers 1987: 50). John Powers, for example, goes on to describe Feck as 'the man who endorses the primacy of love and performs an act of justice on the killer', as the healer from the sixties come to 'redeem eighties' chaos' (ibid.). The problem, of course, is that if Feck lines up on the side of something like an ethical version of the social, then that social has to be defined as loving murderousness. We have to confirm a distinction (and there may be one) between loving and indifferent aggression, loving and indifferent murder – even though this distinction ignores the fact that the object of aggression has, in one decisive sense, remained the same. It is perhaps almost too obvious to state that in both murderous scenarios, a woman is killed, a woman is mourned or not mourned – a repetition, a fixation, which takes us back once more to the image of the dead woman supposed to secure so much for this film. I want to conclude with Judith Williamson's suggestion that *River's Edge* gives us nothing more to respond to than a body we don't know. In fact, the film goes further than this insofar as it repeatedly disinvests the dead girl as a 'nothing' – as, for example, in Matt's ambivalent response when Layne tells him that he has seen Jamie at a party the night before: 'Oh, Jamie, I didn't miss anything, then.' That lack of interest, its disaffection, is then underlined by his refusal simply to call the dead girl a friend. Questioned by the police, Matt will only describe her as 'a friend, I guess' – as the image of the woman's dead body is being played across the screen. At this uncomfortable moment, the film gives us an account of disaffected looking as the symptom of an uncertainty about, a guessing at, what it means to have a friend.

That uncertainty, the ambiguity or inadequacy of symbolization it speaks, immediately bewilders the law for which Jamie 'either was

a friend or she wasn't'. At least in its certainty – either *this* or *that* –
the law is supported by the absolute refusal to prioritize the death
of a woman which defines Layne's desperate attempt to found a
fantasy of group identity ('like Starsky and Hutch') on the concealment of the woman's body: 'She's dead and John's alive. Don't you
see that?' Being a friend to a dead woman, in other words, mourning
her and turning to the law, would only destroy the ties between the
group set up so tenuously over her body. When that group fails, as
it does almost immediately, there is nothing left but the law and the
family – or, to be more specific about the family romance which
governs the end of the film, the brother. In one of the last sequences
of the film, there is an initially unintelligible exchange between Matt
and his younger brother, Tim, when the latter threatens to kill Matt
for having betrayed John. Appealing precisely to the fact that they
are brothers, Matt tries to offset Tim's aggression, repeating 'I'm
your brother' until the younger boy lowers the gun and the camera
holds on their awkward embrace. An affiliation to the friend or to
the group seems to give way here before a fraternal reconciliation –
a reconciliation which has been read as evidence of the film's
'intellectual uncertainty', as proof of its own (fraternal?) affiliation
to the cinematic tradition established by 'Francis Coppola's teen
romances' rather than to the 'punkish malevolence' supposed to
characterize the 'bleak' teen pics (Combs 1987: 294). I suggested in
the previous chapter that at least one of Coppola's 'teen romances'
is not without its own form of malevolence. More relevant here,
though, is a sense that the turn to the figure of the brother at the end
of *River's Edge* is generated by the loss of a metaphoric account of
brotherhood as the privileged instance of the social tie, a loss which
then requires a literalization of that tie, a reinforcement of the name
of brother.

To put this another way: Matt turns to the law and then to the
brother when he finds that he cannot call a woman a friend, when,
as he tells Clarissa why he 'narked' on John, he feels nothing,
however close he looks: 'It got to me. Did it get to you? I kept seeing
her face and how even up that close we didn't feel like we'd lost
anything. That's what got to me the most.' It is, finally, as if a fantasy
of having nothing to lose has somehow moved into the real. Being
up that close, looking closer, makes no difference and only brings
us up against an omission which is felt as intolerable and a misery
doubled precisely insofar as it is lost. Put this way, the recourse to
the figure of the brother is a last resort in the face of a question about

why someone might 'pull a stunt like that' and why, when they do, we don't feel like we've lost anything; it is a key element of the film's final frenzied attempt to close down the logic of violence and omission it is in the process of uncovering. But, and decisively, this tentative and uneasy attempt at cure reinstitutes a now familiar exclusion of the woman which leaves her no place as sister, lover or friend – an exclusion that the film continues to play out, perhaps more mournfully, perhaps by mourning for mourning in its call on the spectator to supply that mourning, through a look at the body of a woman.

Chapter 6

Afterword

'Beyond all shadow of doubt'

In 'The Politics of Friendship', published in 1988, Jacques Derrida suggests that 'all the great ethico-politico-philosophical' discourses on friendship rest on two exclusions: the exclusion of friendship between women and the exclusion of friendship between a man and a woman. This double exclusion, he concludes, confers on that discourse

> the essential and essentially sublime figure of virile homosexuality. Within the familial schema . . . this exclusion privileges the figure of the brother, the name of the brother or the name of brother, more than that of the father – whence the necessity of connecting the political model, especially that of democracy and of the Decalogue, with the rereading of Freud's hypothesis about the alliance of brothers.
>
> (Derrida 1988: 642)

If this is right, then the privileging of the brother at the end of *River's Edge* may be intimately bound up with the film's failure to establish the woman as a friend, as – though this may be the same thing – an object of mourning.[1] At the same time, when he points to the necessity of making the connection between the familial schemas of patriarchy and of democracy and Freud's speculations on the origins of the social tie, Derrida raises the issue of the irreducible confusion that psychoanalysis introduces into the categories of the father and the brother through its rhetorical and conceptual attachment to the figure of Oedipus:

> Heaven bless you, Creon, for this, and make your way
> Smoother than mine has been.
> Where are you, children?

Come, feel your brother's hands. It was their work
That darkened these clear eyes – your father's eyes
As once you knew them, though he never saw
Nor knew what he did when he became your father.
(Sophocles, *Oedipus Rex*: 1513–19; Oedipus, to Ismene and
Antigone)

Something of that confusion is apparent precisely when Freud
attempts to account for the erotic, or lesbian, friendship between two
women in 'The Psychogenesis of a Case of Homosexuality in a
Woman'. In the space of two pages, he finds three different, though
equally certain, sources of the young woman's homosexual object-
choice in a fantasy life rigidly structured by the familial schema of
the Oedipus complex:

> The analysis revealed beyond all shadow of doubt that the lady-
> love was a substitute for – her mother. It is true that the lady
> herself was not a mother, but then she was not the girl's first love.
> The first objects of her affection after the birth of her youngest
> brother were really mothers, women between thirty and thirty-five
> whom she had met with their children during summer holidays or
> in the family circle of acquaintances in town. Motherhood as a *sine
> qua non* in her love object was later on given up, because that
> precondition was difficult to combine in real life with another one,
> which grew more and more important. The specially intense bond
> with her latest love had still another basis which the girl dis-
> covered quite easily one day. Her lady's slender figure, severe
> beauty and downright manner reminded her of the brother who
> was a little older than herself . . . The explanation is as follows . . .
> She became keenly conscious of the wish to have a child, and a
> male one; that what she desired was her father's child and an
> image of him, her consciousness was not allowed to know. And
> what happened next? It was not she who bore the child, but her
> unconsciously hated rival, her mother. Furiously resentful and
> embittered, she turned away from her father and from men
> altogether. After this first great reverse she forswore her woman-
> hood and sought another goal for her libido.
>
> (*PFL* 9: 382–3)

The coincidence between Freud's acknowledgement of the woman's
desire for her mother and his immediate association to, or discovery
of, a fraternal love object whose slender beauty is in direct

opposition to the maternal one, suggests that the elaboration of the sibling bond may be as essential to the attempt to find a different place for the woman in the social and symbolic schemas of psychoanalysis as the reconstruction of the mother–daughter tie which has had such a central place in contemporary feminism.[2] In this case, the brother is there to mediate, more consciously it seems, between the two opposed figures of the unconscious: the Oedipal mother and father fighting for first place in the daughter/sister's fantasy life. At the same time, the elder brother's role in Freud's narrative – after the mother, he is the object of a more intense and somehow aesthetic desire that gives way before the primal and enraging desire for an image of the father – is to bring us back round to the father as the first object for which the homosexual object can then only substitute. That is, the brother puts a brake on a kind of bodily embarrassment, or more strongly, repulsion, which interrupts the attempt to found the woman's homosexuality on a mother-for-mother substitution.[3]

The understanding of fantasy specific to psychoanalysis allows for the displacements and condensations between the different places of father, mother and brother here – and for the indeterminacy of the sister's desire. Freud is explicit that the incompatibility of the mother's body with the daughter's aesthetic valorization of the brother is felt as a problem in 'real life' – not, perhaps, for the daydreaming or fantasmatic scenarios with which psychoanalysis is so frequently working. As such, and crucially, the gesture within Freud's theory which moves to preoccupy femininity with the father and so to dispossess the woman of a certain access to fantasy shows up as a type of blind spot which locks us – women – and the feminized others *into* an interminable oscillation between perversity and narcissism, between the seductive father and Narcissus, and *out of* the profoundly fraternal fantasy of the social tie. At this point, the problem of how to shift the familial or Oedipal schema of psychoanalysis becomes central both to the work of theorizing the feminine in relation to the social or public spheres and to the attempt to replace the vicissitudes of fantasy for the daughter who has become the site of a dereliction of both through her negotiation with the category of the paternal in Freud's theory.

Thus the category of femininity and, though differently, of the woman in the concepts of the collective and of collective fantasy circulating between psychoanalytic, critical and cinematic discourses points to a kind of dislocation which takes various, though not mutually exclusive, forms. Sometimes the woman is making a demand for something for which she should never ask and that bears witness to her deformed relation to both the paternal and the cinematic function. She, and with her the feminized mass spectators of mainstream film, refuses, or is unable to acknowledge, the limit of what can be legitimately asked of the father and his cinematic substitutes. Sometimes she is subject to a clichéd exclusion within, or marginality to, a collective identification which relies on her (self-)annihilation in the name of its seductive fantasies of masculinity and the social alliance. Sometimes the woman occupies the space which opens up between a biological and a symbolic death, between a murder and a failure of mourning. It is a space that, finally, cinema may attempt to fill with the sight of her dead body on film and the reparative, because mournful, spectatorship that body might be supposed to provoke – an attempt at ethics which, like the psychoanalytic and critical discourses used through this book, is then laid open to the threat of its too explicit representation of the exclusion on which it relies.

Notes

2 DADDY'S CINEMA: FEMININITY AND MASS SPECTATORSHIP

1 See, for example, Andreas Huyssen's discussion of the association between femininity and mass culture in 'Mass Culture as Woman: Modernism's Other' (Huyssen 1986). Rachel Bowlby makes the links between femininity and mass consumption in 'The Problem with no Name: Rereading Friedan's *The Feminine Mystique*' (Bowlby 1992).

2 For another feminist critique of the dominance in film theory of the concept of the imaginary as hallucinatory satisfaction see Jacqueline Rose, 'Paranoia and the Film System' (in Penley (ed.) 1988) and the essays on the imaginary and the sexing of visuality in *Sexuality in the Field of Vision* (Rose 1986).

3 FEMININITY, FANTASY AND THE COLLECTIVE (OR *FERRIS BUELLER'S DAY OFF* – TAKE TWO)

1 In *The Freudian Subject*, Mikkel Borch-Jacobsen has demonstrated the impossible double bind structuring the Oedipal law for the boy:

> [T]he law that forbids identification with the Oedipal rival is uttered by the rival with whom one is identifying, and thus it has no legal authority whatever. As a result, there is no choice but to identify with the law that says one must not identify; there is no choice but to imitate . . . the model that says that one must not imitate it; one can only obey it by violating it: not to identify with the father is impossible except on the condition of identifying with him.
>
> (Borch-Jacobsen 1989: 217–18)

What I want to draw attention to in this chapter is the way in which the sexual differentiation of the Oedipus complex, and thus of the Oedipal law, starts to transfer the stress of that double bind onto the feminine form of the superego.

2 Lou Andreas-Salomé's story of Freud's 'charming account of the

"narcissistic" cat' underlines the ambivalence of the narcissism supposed to characterize both the feline and the feminine:

> While Freud maintained his office on the ground floor, the cat had climbed in through the open window. He did not care much for cats or dogs or animals generally, and in the beginning the cat aroused mixed feelings in him, especially when it climbed down from the sofa on which it had made itself comfortable and began to inspect in passing the antique objects which he had placed for the time being on the floor ... But when the cat proceeded to make known its archaeological satisfaction by purring and with its lithe grace did not cause the slightest damage, Freud's heart melted and he ordered milk for it. From then on the cat claimed its rights daily to take a place on the sofa, inspect the antiques and get its bowl of milk. However, despite Freud's increasing affection and admiration, the cat paid him not a bit of attention and coldly turned its green eyes with their slanting pupils towards him as toward any other object ... Finally, after this unequal relationship had lasted a long time without change, one day he found the cat feverish and gasping on the sofa. And although it was most painstakingly treated with hot fomentations and other remedies, it succumbed to pneumonia, leaving naught of itself behind but a symbolic picture of all the peaceful and playful charm of true egoism.
>
> (Andreas-Salomé 1987: 89)

3 Thanks to Rachel Bowlby for her insights into the range of the 'gotta have it'.

4 *RUMBLE FISH*: FRANCIS COPPOLA, SUSAN HINTON AND NARCISSUS

1 Both Carroll and Hinton need to be situated as writers for the youth fiction market. Rosemary Sandberg, an editor of the Fontana Series in 1983, described Hinton's work as a publishing breakthrough: 'It was the first time that alienated or disaffected youth had been looked at by one of their own kind ... *The Outsiders* was the first and the best' (Combs 1983: 239). Richard Combs points to the educational currency enjoyed by Hinton's books as well as her apparent popularity with adolescents in Britain and America. At the same time, like Rose, he associates Hinton with a certain idealization inimical to the realism felt to be so important to the teen fiction market: 'If it doesn't have the ring of truth, teenagers will reject it out of hand.' Combs allows that Hinton may have touched a nerve but

> others in the field, not a few of them journalists, have been broaching a different kind of realism. The American Robert Cormier has produced the widely praised *The Chocolate War*, about a 'high school mafia', and one of British author Jan Needle's books is based on the TV series *Going Out*, about unemployed teenagers.
>
> (ibid.)

Again, two male authors are credited with a different, more authentic relation both to literary realism and to the realism of adolescence.

2 See, for example, Doane 1982; Heath 1986; Johnston 1990; Silverman 1988; Bowlby 1988.

3 I hope to take up elsewhere the way in which that difficulty has also occluded the representation of racial difference in Rivière's paper.

4 The following extract from *Kick* ('Produced by the Kick Organization in the name of Punk') suggests how Bauhaus were received: 'Bauhaus, oh yes Bauhaus. Bela Lugosi Dark Entries Terror Couple. Oh yes. The horror the horror, yes? . . . White on black . . . I asked the questions they told me no lies (nothing is true everything is permitted)' (*Kick* 3, Winter 1980: 3).

5 Kim Newman picks up on *Rumble Fish* as one of the films contributing to a familiar and contemporary nightmare landscape in recent horror films:

> With a little help from *Blade Runner* and the bleak, picturesque vision of Francis Ford Coppola's *Rumble Fish* (1983), these movies create an instantly recognizable universe that has found itself used in an astonishing variety of music videos and unlikely TV commercials for banks and soft drinks. Some apocalypse movies are awful warnings, but these are mainly designed to help the audience stop worrying and, if not love the Bomb, at least find the radioactive ruins as appealing and exotic a locale as the Wild West, the South Seas or Route 66.
>
> (Newman 1988: 87)

This may not be far away from my suggestion that *Rumble Fish* requires something like a suicidal identification with its 'Narcissus' – the Motorcycle Boy (see below).

6 See Laclau and Mouffe 1985; Laclau 1990; Hirst 1986; Heath 1981.

7 There is, of course, a sense in which Freud's theory of the Oedipus complex and the masculine superego is all about turning that possession of and by the other into a type of ideal inheritance for the boy.

5 LOST ANGELS: *RIVER'S EDGE* AND SOCIAL SPECTATORSHIP

1   A classical political dichotomy, not without relevance for feminism, is captured by the question Wilhelm Reich placed at the heart of his dispute with Freud in a conversation with Kurt Eissler in 1952: 'From now onward, the great question arises: *Where does that misery come from?*'

(Rose 1989: 25)

2 The following plot summary helps to clarify the point:

> A young waitress, clothes ripped, bruised, runs screaming from a bar. Sarah Tobias (Foster, excellent) has been gang-raped and her case is taken on by cool and efficient Deputy DA Katheryn Murphy (McGillis). When Murphy makes a deal with the accused men to

reduce the charge to reckless endangerment, Sarah is enraged; and Murphy, beginning to feel the pangs of guilt, decides to prosecute the men who did not take part in the rape but encouraged the others. Surrounded by a storm of controversy – mostly generated by the inclusion of the explicit, some say exploitative, gang-rape scene – the film was written and directed by men, and produced by the Jaffe-Lansing *Fatal Attraction* stable, which hasn't helped its cause.

(Appio 1989: 3)

On the body of the woman as the body of cinema, see Jacqueline Rose's brief discussion of Spike Lee's *Do the Right Thing* (Rose 1989).
3 Mandy Merck discusses *Psycho* as a classic of traumatic vision in Merck 1988. Carol Clover also draws attention to the comments made by the cult horror film director, Dario Argento (who seems to confirm Rose's analysis – see previous note): '"I like women, especially beautiful ones. If they have a good face and figure, I would much prefer to watch them being murdered than an ugly girl or a man"' (Clover 1989: 111).

6 AFTERWORD: 'BEYOND ALL SHADOW OF DOUBT'

1 At the same time, as one critic has noted, disapprovingly, the reinforce-ment of the brother allows the 'name of the father' back in on the margin of the film. The police officer who questioned Matt earlier in the film is in on these final scenes but he is now treated with 'excessive politeness and respect' (Rapping 1988: 19). Thus the devastating critique of the family which runs through *River's Edge* may start to be reinflected in the last few frames of the film.
2 See, for example, Irigaray 1985 and Whitford 1991. Juliet Flower MacCannell has made a related point in her analysis of political modernity as a 'régime of the brother': 'If the sister is missing in modernity's family romance, it is because her mother has never occupied the symbolic position, has never herself been able to be a superego for her daughter' (MacCannell 1991: 145)
3 Freud is explicit about the embarrassment felt by pregnant mothers with their teenage daughters: 'In such circumstances mothers with daughters of nearly a marriageable age usually feel embarrassed in regard to them, while the daughters are apt to feel for their mothers a mixture of compassion, contempt and envy which does nothing to increase their tenderness for them' (*PFL* 9: 383).

Bibliography

Unless otherwise indicated in the text all references to Freud's work can be found in *The Pelican Freud Library*, Harmondsworth: Penguin.

Abel, E. (1990) 'Race, Class, and Psychoanalysis? Opening Questions', in M. Hirsch and E. Keller (eds), *Conflicts in Feminism*, London: Routledge.

Abraham, N. and Torok, M. (1980) 'Introjection and Incorporation: Mourning or Melancholia', in S. Lebovici and D. Widlocher (eds), *Psychoanalysis in France*, New York: International Universities Press.

—— (1986) *The Wolf Man's Magic Word*, trans. N. Rand, Minneapolis: Minnesota University Press.

Abramson, P. (1987) 'Bitter Memories of Murder: A Movie Reopens Old Wounds in a California Town', in *Newsweek*, 22 June.

Adair, G. (1983) 'The Incisive Fossa: *The Outsiders*', in *Sight and Sound* 52 (4).

Adorno, T. (1991) *The Culture Industry*, ed. J.M. Bernstein, London: Routledge.

Adorno, T. and Horkheimer, M. (1979) *Dialectic of Enlightenment*, trans. John Cumming, London: Verso. First published in 1944.

Andreas-Salomé, L. (1987) *The Freud Journal*, London: Quartet Books.

Ansen, D. (1983) 'Coppola Courts the Kiddies', in *Newsweek*, 4 April.

Appignanesi, L. and Forrester, J. (1992) *Freud's Women*, London: Weidenfeld and Nicolson.

Appio, I. (1989) Review of *The Accused*, in *The Time Out Film Guide*, ed. T. Milne, Harmondsworth: Penguin.

Auty, C. (1984) 'Tightrope Act: *Rumble Fish*', in *Sight and Sound* 53 (2).

Barrett, M. and McIntosh, M. (1982), 'Narcissism and the Family: A Critique of Lasch', in *New Left Review* 135.

Benjamin, J. (1978) 'Authority and the Family Revisited', in *New German Critique* 13.

Bergstrom, J. and Doane, M.A. (1989) 'The Female Spectator: Contexts and Directions', in 'The Spectatrix', *Camera Obscura* 20–1.

Bernstein, J.M. (ed.) (1991) 'Introduction' to T. Adorno, *The Culture Industry*, London: Routledge.

Billson, A. (1989) Review of *The Breakfast Club*, in *The Time Out Film Guide*, ed. T. Milne, Harmondsworth: Penguin.

'Bookworm' (1991) *Punch*, April.

Borch-Jacobsen, M. (1989) *The Freudian Subject*, trans. C. Porter, London: Macmillan.

—— (1991) 'The Freudian Subject: From Politics to Ethics', trans. R. Miller, in E. Cadava *et al.* (eds), *Who Comes After the Subject?*, London: Routledge.

Bowlby, R. (1988) *Virginia Woolf: Feminist Destinations*, Oxford: Blackwell.

—— (1992) *Still Crazy After All These Years*, London/New York: Routledge.

Chasseguet-Smirgel, J. (1985) *The Ego Ideal*, London: Free Association Books.

Chodorow, N. (1978) *The Reproduction of Mothering: Psychoanalysis and the Sociology of Gender*, Berkeley: University of California Press.

Clover, C. (1989) 'Her Body, Himself: Gender in the Slasher Film', in J. Donald (ed.), *Fantasy and Cinema*, London: The British Film Institute.

Combs, R. (1983) 'Why I Enjoyed Reading *The Outsiders*', in *Monthly Film Bulletin* 50 (596).

—— (1987) '*River's Edge*', in *Monthly Film Bulletin* 50, 645.

Copjec, J. (1989) 'The Orthopsychic Subject: Film Theory and the Reception of Lacan', in *October* 49.

Corliss, R. (1983a) 'Playing Tough, Going Nowhere', in *Time*, 4 April.

—— (1983b) 'Time Bomb: *Rumble Fish*', in *Time*, 24 October.

Cowie, E. (1978) 'Woman as Sign', in *m/f* 1.

Creed, B. (1988) 'A Journey Through *Blue Velvet*: Film, Fantasy and the Female Spectator', in *New Formations* 6.

Davidson, A. (1984) 'The Assault on Freud', in *London Review of Books* 6 (12).

Derrida, J. (1984) 'No Apocalypse, Not Now (Full Speed Ahead, Seven Missiles, Seven Missives)', trans. C. Porter and P. Lewis, in *Diacritics* 14 (2).

—— (1987) *The Post Card*, trans. A. Bass, Chicago: Chicago University Press.

—— (1988) 'The Politics of Friendship', trans. G. Motzkin, in *The Journal of Philosophy*, 85 (11).

Dinnerstein, D. (1978) *The Mermaid and the Minotaur*, USA: Harper and Row.

Doane, M.A. (1982) 'Film and the Masquerade: Theorizing the Female Spectator', in *Screen* 23 (3/4).

—— (1987) *The Desire to Desire: The Woman's Film of the 1940s*, London: Macmillan.

Doherty, T. (1988) *Teenagers and Teenpics: The Juvenilization of American Movies in the 1950s*, London: Unwin Hyman.

Ellis, B. Easton. (1985) *Less than Zero*, London: Pan Macmillan.

—— (1991) *American Psycho*, London: Pan Macmillan.

Fargier, J-P. (1971) 'Parenthesis or Indirect Route: An Attempt at a Theoretical Definition of the Relationship between Cinema and Politics', in *Screen* 12 (2).

Flett, K. (1989) 'Hollywood's Golden Girl', in *The Face* 2 (4).

Freud, S. (1953–74) *The Standard Edition of the Complete Psychological Works of Sigmund Freud*, 24 volumes, trans. and ed. by James Strachey, London: The Hogarth Press.

—— (1973–86) *The Pelican Freud Library*, 15 volumes, trans. and ed. by James Strachey, general editor: Angela Richards, Harmondsworth: Penguin.

—— (1933) 'Femininity', in *New Introductory Lectures*, trans. and ed. James Strachey, in The International Psycho-Analytical Library 24, ed. Masud R. Khan, London: The Hogarth Press.

—— (1963) *Freud: Therapy and Technique*, ed. P. Rieff, New York: Macmillan.

—— (1987) *A Phylogenetic Fantasy: Overview of the Transference Neuroses*, ed. I. Grubrich-Simitis, Cambridge, Massachusetts and London, England: The Belknap Press of Harvard University Press.

Friedan, B. (1963) *The Feminine Mystique*, New York: Dell Publishing Company.

Goldman, S. (1989) Review of *Ferris Bueller's Day Off* in *The Time Out Film Guide*, ed. T. Milne, Harmondsworth: Penguin.

Grossberg, L. (1988) 'Rockin' with Reagan, or the Mainstreaming of Postmodernity', in *Cultural Critique* 10.

Hansen, M. (1981–2) 'Co-operative Auteur Cinema and the Oppositional Public Sphere', in *New German Critique* 24–5.

—— (1986) 'Pleasure, Ambivalence and Identification: Valentino and Female Spectatorship', in *Cinema Journal* 25 (4).

Harmetz, A. (1987) '*River's Edge* Defies Experts' Expectations', in *The New York Times*, 6 June.

Heath, S. (1981) *Questions of Cinema*, London: Macmillan.

—— (1986) 'Joan Rivière and the Masquerade', in V. Burgin, J. Donald and C. Kaplan (eds), *Formations of Fantasy*, London: Methuen.

Heilpern, J. (1990) 'Dressed to Kill and Bound for the Best-seller Lists', in *The Independent on Sunday*, 25 November.

Hinton, S.E. (1977) *Rumble Fish*, London: HarperCollins.

Hirst, P. (1986) 'Althusser's Theory of Ideology', in *Economy and Society* 5 (4).

Hudson, C. (1991) 'Pass the Chic Bag', in *Evening Standard*, 7 March.

Hunter, T. (1987) 'Sneaking up on Howard Hawks', interview in *Monthly Film Bulletin* 54 (645).

Huyssen, A. (1986) *After the Great Divide: Modernism, Mass Culture, Postmodernism*, London: Macmillan.

Irigaray, L. (1985) *Speculum of the Other Woman*, trans. G.C. Gill, New York: Cornell University Press.

Jameson, F. (1984) 'Postmodernism or the Cultural Logic of Late Capitalism', in *New Left Review* 146.

Johnston, C. (1990) 'Femininity and the Masquerade: *Anne of the Indies*', in E.A. Kaplan (ed.), *Psychoanalysis and Cinema*, London/New York: Routledge.

Johnston, S. (1983) '*The Outsiders*', in *Monthly Film Bulletin* 50 (596).

—— (1984) '*Rumble Fish*', in *Monthly Film Bulletin* 51 (600).

Kracauer, S. (1972) 'Caligari', in *The Cabinet of Dr. Caligari: A Film by*

Robert Wiene, trans. and description of action by R.V. Adkinson, London: Lorrimer Publishing Ltd.

Kristeva, J. (1986a) 'Women's Time', in T. Moi (ed.), *The Kristeva Reader*, Oxford: Basil Blackwell.

—— (1986b) 'Freud and Love: Treatment and its Discontents', in T. Moi (ed.), *The Kristeva Reader*, Oxford: Basil Blackwell.

—— (1987) *Tales of Love*, trans. Leon S. Roudiez, New York: Columbia University Press.

Kroll, J. (1983) 'Coppola's Teen-Age Inferno', in *Newsweek*, 7 November.

Kuhn, A. (1989) Contribution to 'The Spectatrix', *Camera Obscura* 20–1.

Lacan, J. (1977) *Ecrits: A Selection*, trans. A. Sheridan, London: Tavistock.

—— (1979) *The Four Fundamental Concepts of Psycho-Analysis*, trans. A. Sheridan, Harmondsworth: Penguin.

Laclau, E. (1990) *New Reflections on the Revolution of Our Time*, London: Verso.

Laclau, E. and Mouffe, C. (1985) *Hegemony and Socialist Strategy*, London: Verso.

Lacoue-Labarthe, P. and Nancy, J-L. (1989) 'The Unconscious is Destructured Like an Affect', trans. B. Holmes, in *The Stanford Literary Review* 6.

Laplanche, J. (1976) *Life and Death in Psychoanalysis*, trans. Jeffrey Mehlman, Baltimore: The Johns Hopkins Press.

Laplanche, J. and Pontalis, J-B. (1986) 'Fantasy and the Origins of Sexuality', in V. Burgin, J. Donald and C. Kaplan (eds), *Formations of Fantasy*, London: Methuen. First published in 1964.

—— (1973) *The Language of Psychoanalysis*, London: The Institute of Psychoanalysis/Karnac Books.

Lasch, C. (1980) *The Culture of Narcissism: American Life in an Age of Diminishing Expectations*, London: Abacus.

—— (1981) 'The Freudian Left', in *New Left Review* 129.

—— (1985) 'Introduction' to J. Chasseguet-Smirgel, *The Ego Ideal*, London: Free Association Books.

Lévi-Strauss, C. (1969) *The Elementary Structures of Kinship*, trans. J. Bell, J. von Sturmer and R. Needham, Boston: Beacon Press. First published in 1949.

Liebman, S. (1988) 'On New German Cinema, Art, Enlightenment and the Public Sphere: An Interview with Alexander Kluge', in *October* 46.

Marcus, G. (1985) '*Less Than Zero*', in *Artforum*, September.

Masson, J.M. (1984) *Freud: The Assault on Truth*, London: Faber & Faber.

Mayne, J. (1993) *Cinema and Spectatorship*, London/New York: Routledge.

MacCannell, J. Flower (1991) *The Régime of the Brother: After the Patriarchy*, London: Routledge.

McGuire, W. (ed.) (1974) *The Freud–Jung Letters*, trans. R. Manheim and R.F.C. Hull, London: The Hogarth Press and RKP.

McRobbie, A. (1991) *Feminism and Youth Culture*, London: Macmillan.

Merck, M. (1988) 'Bedroom Horror: The Fatal Attraction of *Intercourse*', in *Feminist Review* 30.

Milne, T. (ed.) (1989) *The Time Out Film Guide*, Harmondsworth: Penguin.

Modleski, T. (1988) 'Three Men and Baby M', in *Camera Obscura* 17.

Mulvey, L. (1975) 'Visual Pleasure and Narrative Cinema', in *Screen* 16 (3).
—— (1981) 'Afterthoughts on "Visual Pleasure and Narrative Cinema" inspired by *Duel in the Sun*', in *Framework* 15–17.
—— (1989) Contribution to 'The Spectatrix', *Camera Obscura* 20–1.
Negt, O. and Kluge, A. (1988), 'The Public Sphere and Experience', in *October* 46.
Newman, K. (1988) *Nightmare Movies: A Critical History of the Horror Movie from 1968*, London: Bloomsbury Publishing Ltd.
Packard, V. (1957) *The Hidden Persuaders*, USA: David McKay.
Peachment, C. (1989) Review of *Rumble Fish*, in *The Time Out Film Guide*, ed. T. Milne, Harmondsworth: Penguin.
Penley, C. (ed.) (1988) *Feminism and Film Theory*, New York: Routledge.
—— (1989a) *The Future of an Illusion: Film, Feminism, and Psychoanalysis*, London/New York: Routledge.
—— (1989b) Contribution to 'The Spectatrix', *Camera Obscura* 20–1.
Pfeil, F. (1989) *Another Tale to Tell*, London: Verso.
Porter, V. (1985) *On Cinema*, London: Pluto Press.
Powdermaker, H. (1950) *Hollywood the Dream Factory: An Anthropologist Looks at the Movie Makers*, London: Secker and Warburg.
Powers, J. (1987) 'Bleak Chic', in *American Film* 12 (5).
Pye, M. (1986) 'Young and Blank and Credit-carded', in *The Observer*, 9 February.
Rapping, E. (1988) 'Hollywood's Youth Cult Films', in *Cineaste* 16.
Riesman, D. (1950) *The Lonely Crowd*, Newhaven: Yale University Press.
Rivière, J. (1986) 'Womanliness as a Masquerade', in V. Burgin, J. Donald and C. Kaplan (eds), *Formations of Fantasy*, London: Methuen.
Rose, C. (1983) 'The Fiction of S.E. Hinton', in *Monthly Film Bulletin* 50 (596).
Rose, J. (1986) *Sexuality in the Field of Vision*, London: Verso.
—— (1989) "Where Does the Misery Come From?": Psychoanalysis, Feminism and the Event', in R. Feldstein and J. Roof (eds), *Feminism and Psychoanalysis*, Ithaca: Cornell University Press.
Rubin, G. (1975) 'The Traffic in Women', in R. Reiter (ed.), *Toward an Anthropology of Women*, New York: Monthly Review Press.
Ryan, M. and Kellner, D. (1990) *Camera Politica: The Politics and Ideology of Contemporary Hollywood Film*, Bloomington: Indiana University Press.
Segal, H. (1987) 'Silence is Not the Real Crime', in *International Review of Psychoanalysis* 14 (3).
Seiter, E. (1989) Contribution to 'The Spectatrix', *Camera Obscura* 20–1.
Silverman, K. (1988) 'Masochism and Male Subjectivity', in *Camera Obscura* 17.
Simon, J. (1987) 'Will Kids be Kids?', in *National Review*, 19 January.
Spratt, M. (1984) 'Rebels, Rumbles and Motorcycle Boys', in *Cinema Papers* 48.
Stacey, J. (1987) 'Desperately Seeking Difference', in *Screen* 28 (1).
Steedman, C. (1986) *Landscape for a Good Woman*, London: Virago.
Toffler, A. (1970) *Future Shock*, London: Pan Books/The Bodley Head.

Whitford, M. (1991) *Luce Irigaray: Philosophy in the Feminine*, London: Routledge.
Whyte, W.H. (1956) *The Organization Man*, New York: Simon & Schuster.
Williamson, J. (1987) 'The Matter with Kids Today', in *New Statesman*, 16 October.
Winnicott, D. (1986) 'Fear of Breakdown', in G. Kohon (ed.), *The British School of Psychoanalysis: The Independent Tradition*, London: Free Association Books.
Woolf, V. (1928) *Orlando: A Biography*, London: The Hogarth Press.
Zižek, S. (1989) *The Sublime Object of Ideology*, London: Verso.

Index